D1474893

THE FUTURE REMEMBERED

Loyola Lecture Series
in Political Analysis

Richard Shelly Hartigan
EDITOR AND DIRECTOR

The Future Remembered

An Essay in Biopolitics

RICHARD SHELLY HARTIGAN

University of Notre Dame Press
Notre Dame, Indiana

Library of Congress Cataloging-in-Publication Data

Hartigan, Richard Shelly.
   The future remembered.

   (Loyola lecture series in political analysis)
   Bibliography: p.
   Includes index.
   1. Biopolitics. 2. Man. I. Title. II. Series.
JA80.H37 1988   320'.01'574   87-40345
ISBN 0-268-00972-4

Manufactured in the United States of America

FOR NANCY
AND OUR CHILDREN,
PAT, TIM, JENNY AND BETH

Contents

Acknowledgments

In 1982 my colleagues in the Political Science Department suggested that I give the eighth presentation of the Loyola Lectures in Political Analysis. This volume, in much altered form, grew from those lectures. I am indebted to them for their vote of confidence in me, and to Professor James Wiser, in particular, who played the devil's advocate as I later wrestled with these ideas.

Much needed time to complete this project was afforded me by Loyola University of Chicago in the form of a semester leave of absence, and by the Earhart Foundation with a summer research grant. To both institutions, I am very grateful, especially to Ronald E. Walker, Dean of Faculties at the former, and Antony T. Sullivan at the latter.

The friends and scholars at other institutions, and in disciplines as varied as history, anthropology, and marine geology, who have offered advice and criticism as this work took shape, are too many to name individually. They know who they are and, I hope, how deeply I appreciate their support. A special thanks is due to a fellow practitioner, Professor Joseph Losco of Ball State University, whose critical reading of the manuscript has helped me to clarify and correct a number of my arguments, and to my graduate student, Diane Kondratowicz, whose practiced feminist eye has hopefully saved me from some thoroughly unintended appearances of sexism. Special appreciation is also due to Konrad Lorenz and the late Robert Ardrey who both, in their own ways, inspired and encouraged a young scholar many years ago.

James Langford, Director of the University of Notre Dame Press, has patiently supported this work, while

Margaret Kranzfelder has patiently typed endless revisions. Most patient has been my wife Nancy who has endured my dinnertime lectures and leavened them with wit and perception. Thanks to you all.

Introduction

An anonymous genius once observed that if one thing is certain about the human being it is its tendency to reinvent the wheel. Nowhere is the truth of this adage more apparent than in philosophies of and about ourselves, or more specifically, human nature theory.

Unlike the natural sciences, in which a steady accumulation of knowledge occurs, theories of human nature seem to run in recurring cycles, falling in and out of fashion but with no apparent "net gain" in truth about the subject. Indeed, one may come away from a survey of Western political philosophy with the impression that the dominant ideas of any period have attained their rank according to who could shout the loudest. Intellectual movements, ideologies, and assorted world-views command adherence for a time and are then swept aside by reaction, only to surface again in some altered form. There seems to be nothing new under the sun when it comes to theories of human nature.

Such a conclusion is, of course, a gross oversimplification. Each era attempts a new synthesis of expanded knowledge with older truths, but not always with the same degree of success. What constitutes a net gain in the philosophy of human nature is the staying power which certain ideas exhibit. They continue to recommend themselves over time, even when the "Grand theories" of which they were a part are no longer satisfactory.

What each new age encounters are insights from the past, sparks of imagination that warrant reexamination in the light of new discovery. Such a period is once again upon us in the presence of the biological revolution.

Without fear of hyperbole it can be stated that our knowledge of living organisms has taken a quantum leap in the last thirty years. One instance among many, the unraveling of the genetic code, is enough to mark this time as one of the most important in human history. And the momentum of discovery in all areas of the life sciences is increasing at an accelerated rate and on a daily basis.

The effects of this explosion of knowledge have not been confined to the natural sciences. Social scientists and humanists have become increasingly aware that they can no longer remain insulated from a range of scientific data which is continually demanding a reassessment of the way in which we define ourselves. Just as the natural sciences are dismantling the boundaries which have separated them one from another, true humanists, regardless of the discipline with which they align themselves, are discovering common ground with each other, as well as with the "hard" sciences.[1] A new synthesis is underway that seeks understanding of the real and total being—a holistic picture of ourselves in place of the one-dimensional abstraction of, for example, "economic" or "political" models of humanity. One mark of this effort is the establishment of a field of study called "human ethology"—the study of *Homo sapiens* in its natural habitat, broadly defined.[2]

My own present identification is with a somewhat less ambitious endeavor, though one which aims at this larger target—the field of biopolitics. As the name implies, it is an attempt to study the traditionally accepted areas of the "political" person from the broader perspective of evolutionary biology and the life sciences. If further specification is required, I would be forced to say that the following essay is an effort in biopolitical philosophy or evolutionary ethics, since I am specifically addressing ethical and philosophical issues within the context of evolutionary theory. If these terms seem daunting, even pretentious, it is unavoidable, given the present demarcations of academic disciplines. No one will be happier than I to eventually submerge myself in a grand discipline of human ethology, along with biohistorians, biosociologists, biophilosophers, political anthropologists, and others.

In this essay I am attempting to confront the reality of human value systems from the perspective of evolutionary biology. Seen within this context, it is logical to conclude that, whereas we correctly describe ourselves as normative, rule-making and abiding beings, the source of that characteristic is far more primordial than we have yet realized. It is likely that our "normativeness" is not only as fundamental to our biological programming as our linguistic ability, but far more ancient. If this is so, and, since our verbal powers originate from our big brain—an infant organ only half a million years old—it further follows that we were normative animals long before we could give articulation to the rules which bound us together. With these and other considerations relevant to this perspective, how we define our nature, and all that follows from that accordance, may require substantial revision. Let me hasten to add that I do not presume to "prove" the biological origins of human values in this short space. But if my presentation, taken as a whole, is sufficiently plausible to convince others that this perspective must be pursued, and that within it, my arguments make sense, then I will be satisfied.

The question of the nature and origin of our species has intrigued philosophers in the West for over two thousand years. During this time various explanations and definitions have been offered, from the metaphysical to the materialist, with all shades in between. But the specific question of the origin of *Homo sapiens'* normative control over itself has usually remained unasked, as though its answer were implicitly contained in the larger definitions themselves. Thus Christianity has implied that the question is irrelevant, given the presumption of a divine creator of and lawgiver to its supreme creation. Among modern secular theories of human nature, including both Liberal and Marxist traditions, the assumption has been that human values have evolved from reasoned necessity and economic pressures and, as such, are perpetuated as custom, convention, and tradition. True as this may be at a secondary level of human experience in place and over time, it does not answer a prior question: "If so, who teaches the teacher?" Put differently, we may ask why human societies, admittedly composed of creatures who affect and are affected by their environment, nonetheless demonstrate consistent adherence to a few fundamental normative principles?

It is important to pose these puzzles more explicitly, and now in the light of an enormously expanded scientific knowledge of what we are as organisms. This more accurate understanding of what we are does not imply what we *must* become nor what we *ought* to do. It does provide us with the wherewithal to appreciate what we are capable of attaining, should we so choose.

I

The Query and the Quest

Know then thyself, presume
not God to scan,
The proper study of
mankind is man.

Alexander Pope
An Essay on Man

The quest to know ourselves is a task that we assumed at
the dawn of our dim beginnings as reflective creatures.
Alone among living things, we ask the question, "What are
we?" In itself this means that we know we are different,
unique. Observation plus reflection reminds us constantly
of our special qualities and abilities. We can transform the
world around us, even escape the very planet that we
inhabit. We can store and transmit our complex knowledge
and imagination. And we can even permanently extinguish
all life, if we choose to do so, with weapons of our own
making. All this and more reminds us of the enormous
gulf that separates our being from others.

Once noted, however, why bother to inquire further?
That is, why speculate as to the reason or reasons for our
uniqueness as a species? Why not take it for granted and
proceed? A partial answer is contained in the question:
The very reason we are what we are demands that we
inquire about *what* we are. There can be no other way. We
are reflective and hence must be self-reflective. We are
imaginative and must therefore imagine what we may be.
We are inquisitive and so are bound to inquire about our
origins and destinies.

Sometimes consciously, most often intuitively, we understand the relationship between what we are and why we believe and act as we do. We "know" that our actions have causes and that those causes are rooted in our being. To know what we do, to understand why we act or respond as we do, we perceive that we must first determine causes which can only have their source in our humanness, our nature. And so we seek to define ourselves in our separateness, and we create theories of human nature.

These theories about what we are, as individuals and as a species, have ranged widely, reflecting in their variety the differences among their authors. We have described ourselves as everything from a near-sublime reflection of God with infinite potential for virtue to a troglodyte beast predetermined by our limited capacities and doomed to a life of vice. This very spectrum of views does at least verify that we are imaginative when it comes to self-analysis and definition.

Implicit in this questioning as to our nature or essence is that somehow a knowledge of what we are will reveal what we ought to do. We seem plagued as thinking beings with the malady of self-doubt. We constantly question our motives for doing what we do and we seek to justify ourselves before and after our actions. This "oughtness" in our lives consistently bothers us. It reminds us of past omissions or commissions, of fantasies fulfilled or unfulfilled, of demons exorcised or still to be faced, of challenges met or yet to be encountered. Throughout our lives we ask ourselves, "Should I?"

Linked with our desire to understand ourselves (and an intuition that until we do, we possess little guide as to what we should do) is the desire for that final dimension of certainty, of surety that what we think about ourselves is really true. All of our reflection and consequent ethical speculation may be meaningless unless we have confidence that what we think we know is indeed the truth. Without this assurance, how we name ourselves and what we require of ourselves is irrelevant.

To the earlier question of why we embark on the quest of self-knowledge, the tentative answer is because the very nature which we seek to explain and define prescribes that we do so. The gain of such an effort appears to have both a self-gratifying result—knowledge which satisfies our urge to know—and a practical advantage—that knowledge serves as a guide for how we ought to act. But precisely because we are (or can characterize ourselves as) thinking, imaginative, inquisitive beings, we strive for verification of our knowledge, justification that our ideas are not fantasy and that our actions have meaning.

These prefatory remarks themselves represent a tentative human nature theory. I have briefly described myself and my conspecifics as having several characteristics: an ability to think or reason (whatever that may be) to an understanding of what we are, so as to determine what we are able to do, while all the time fraught with doubt that what we presume to know is actually true. I have described in this short space some of those wonts and wants that I ascribe to myself and my species. With a slight bow to Descartes, if I can reason about my nature, it must be of my nature to do so.

Until recently formal philosophizing about human nature had fallen from fashion, while much of the vocabulary of traditional philosophy became obsolete or archaic in light of the natural sciences.[3] Of what relevance is it to use such general terms as "nature," "substance" or "essence" when the physical sciences speak to us in terms of molecules, atoms, and quarks? As new findings blur the distinctions among the sciences of biology, physics, and chemistry, as we learn daily that our human behavior and institutions are not so unique as we once thought but are similar, even identical, to other animals, we correctly question the effort to distinguish natures. If we are of one living bulk, different from each other only by degrees of molecular quantity, it seems absurd to presume an essential quality in man which makes him (or any other species) special. To these and other like arguments I can only accede. Yet, I still feel bound to follow the exhortation of Socrates—to at least try to know myself.

The ancient Greek tragedians often warned against the pitfall of hubris, that overweening presumption that led heroes to imitate or defy the gods. Modern humans, with more faith in science than in the gods, deem such pride to be a virtue, not a vice. Hence, the quest for self-knowledge and realization, begun two thousand years ago by Socrates, continues unabated, now aided by the formidable tools of modern science.

When the philosophers of the past queried about human nature they assumed much, but, most of all, that human nature was unique. For the Christian, God's ultimate creation was a fallen but redeemable species, made in the image and likeness of the creator, different from and set above all other creatures, great or small. For the philosophers of the Enlightenment, the ability to reason set humans apart from other animals and represented an unbridgeable gulf between their natures. Only since Darwin have we come to fully acknowledge that which Aristotle had merely glimpsed —*Homo sapiens*, though certainly different from other life forms, is radically at one with them as well. Our task of self-investigation now requires that we seek our uniqueness through our sameness with other species, our divergence from them to be revealed in our unity with them.

With this enlarged perspective our familiar vocabulary will not always be adequate to our new task of analysis and description. The specialist of the modern life sciences moves easily through a verbal labyrinth of terminology. "Ontogeny" and "haplodiploidy," "phenotypic" and "homozygous" are words with precise meanings that transcend the barriers of different languages. By contrast, the vocabulary of the philosophy of human nature has changed little since the days of its inception, due in large part to its increasing isolation from the natural sciences. A new, holistic view of our species, a view which seeks an understanding of the organism from its biologic base, offers the promise of a new synthesis of study—and withall, an end to the Babel used to describe the being. But, until that welcome day finally dawns, philosophers must continue to rely, at least to some extent, on words they know to be imprecise —if only because they are familiar.

Virtually every historic view of how human beings should behave toward their fellowman or woman—their "conspecific"—has been based on a theory of human nature. These views are as varied as the authors and their experiences, but they share a common characteristic—inevitably they are self-justifying. From them have sprung history's crusades and jihads, holocausts and apartheids, castes and classes, and levels in heaven or hell. Political and economic systems, foreign policies, and ideologies of every stripe are claimed as the logical extension or perfect reflection of a true view of humanity. How persons see and understand themselves as human has determined their reactions to their kin, their immediate social group, and societies other than their own.

For over two thousand years the Western philosophical tradition has been especially preoccupied with the quest to define human nature. Since Socrates' first rhetorical inquiry, followed by his exhortation to know oneself, his intellectual kindred spirits have provided an array of answers to the queries "What does it mean to be human, why do we behave as we do, and how ought we to act?"

Socrates' student Plato described human nature as tripartite, being composed of reason, spirit, and appetite. A balance of these characteristics in both the individual and his society would produce both a just person and a just *polis* or political community. From his premises, Plato logically concluded a policy recommendation—perpetual rule by a self-perpetuating elite.

Plato's student, in turn, declared his teacher's ideal inadequate, even false. More cautious, more inclined to look at humankind with all of its warts and flaws, more interested in the non-human life around him than Plato, Aristotle laid a foundation of thought which in many respects is still attractive today. He argued that humans are a special kind of animal but an animal nonetheless. They are creatures capable of rational thought and discourse who reside in a social structure that is both the product and the source of their own contrivance. He called this structure the *polis.*

What distinguishes Aristotle from Plato most sharply is the former's greater reliance on what we today call the empirical or scientific method. Plato observed humans in action but largely to confirm his preconceived conclusions; Aristotle gathered data from which he drew his conclusions. The difference in approach is best described as the distinction between deductive or *a priori* reasoning (Plato) and inductive or *a posteriori* reasoning (Aristotle). The distinction is a crucial one upon which my own analyses rely.

For the natural scientist-philosopher Aristotle, policy recommendations for how humans ought to construct their political communities were tempered by his belief that the matter of nature was still an open question. From his own observations, he concluded that the most secure *polis* was one in which many factors (pride, amity, greed, lust, reason) were balanced among individuals and classes. Implicit in his stated preference for a predominantly middle-class polity, however, was his admission that further investigation would reveal as yet unknown facts which would require revision of his own conclusions. Aristotle was the first systematic philosopher who based his analysis of human nature on observable, sense-perceived data and hence recognized that no final conclusions about the being could be drawn until all the facts about it were known.

The next great intellect to postulate a human nature theory was the fourth-century Bishop of Hippo, St. Augustine. Influenced by neo-Platonic philosophy, imbued with a confident Christian faith and zeal, Augustine, too, has retained a certain authority in Western thought. In his view humanity is fundamentally inclined toward evil, a condition predetermined by the fall from grace of Adam and Eve. Their original hubris destined them and their offspring to a life of sin and ultimate perdition. The evils that humans wrought upon themselves and each other could be explained by this precondition. Only the intervention of Jesus, the son of God, bringing with him the promise of divine forgiveness, would alleviate humans' suffering and permit them to transcend their nature.

For Augustine, this nature was fixed or static in its relationship and origin to its creator; only the creator's magnanimity could enable persons to alter their status. Finally, the only connection between the human and the rest of living beings lay in the fact that all life owed its origin to the same creator. In all other respects they shared little in common. Since God as author ruled the universe, humans as his highest (though temporarily fallen) creation ruled the rest of nature. By analogy, this hierarchy should obtain within human societies as well where some were born to rule and others to serve.

In this survey, two thinkers summarize the abandonment of medieval dogmatism. Both Machiavelli in the fifteenth century and Thomas Hobbes in the seventeenth departed sharply from the religious orientation of the earlier tradition and expounded a radically secular view of human nature. For them, individuals were driven to be aggressive and to exert power over each other. Whether or not this was a legacy of original sin was not their concern. In this respect they were of the school of Aristotle in that they reported what they observed and drew the logical conclusions. Both reasoned that order was better than chaos for individual and group survival, and that force was necessary to bring about and maintain that order. Thus came Machiavelli's recommendation of a wily prince who could act as a lion or a fox as the situation required, and Hobbes's insistence on an absolute ruler in a Leviathan state.

The one-dimensional view of humanity held by both writers ironically led them to conclusions regarding the best structure for society not unlike those of Plato and Augustine. Yet at the same time, both proclaimed their methods of investigation to be empirical and observational, that is, more akin to Aristotle's way of thinking.

John Locke was the unwitting author of a number of errors in modern social philosophy.[4] In the seventeenth century Locke asserted a one-dimensional view of human nature opposite from that of Hobbes or Machiavelli. Whereas the latter two asserted that humans' generally accepted nasty characteristics reflected their real selves, Locke countered that the true nature of the species was benign, generous, loving, and cooperative. He concluded that, given a voice in how they were governed, these basic human traits would reveal themselves and prevail. But, whereas Hobbes and Machiavelli intended to base their theories on observation and evidence, Locke's arguments relied largely on vague and unspecified, non-demonstrable generalities. Thus, while claiming fidelity to the Cartesian methodology, this foremost exponent of modern representative government actually relied on rhetorical *a priori* assumptions to make his case. His conclusions, no matter how attractive, could no more claim a scientific or factual support than could Plato's quite opposite ones—and for precisely the same reason.

What Locke bequeathed to modern social theory was a naive confidence that human beings themselves, not God or some ephemeral notion of nature, were masters of their destinies because they alone possessed a rational capacity to understand their environment and the ability to alter it to their will. I call this the syndrome of the "disembodied, rational eyeball," the myth which pictures a creature as endowed with a superior intelligence and unencumbered by any instincts or necessary connection with the rest of nature. Locke's person can change its environment to suit its needs or desires, can infinitely progress to a better life or condition, and can eradicate all ills which it perceives. His view of human nature is not unlike the Augustinian-Christian tradition in that it exalts humanity while implicitly diminishing all other existence. The difference between the two presumptions is that Locke had secularized the source of this superiority, that is, he effectively eliminated a personal divine source for it. The human being is its own, Locke seems to say, and what a glorious creature it is!

To link modern human nature theorists with Locke may seem gratuitous since their premises and conclusions are so often different from his. Closer scrutiny reveals, however, that among others, Marx and Freud share some fundamental assumptions with Locke. Both believe that human nature is basically "good," that is, cooperative, docile, benign; both hold that what is distasteful in human behavior is the result of extraneous forces or circumstances; and finally, both agree that the individual itself can change its situation for the better if only it awakens to the need for and the way of change. The influence of these two thinkers on contemporary political and social theory and practice needs no elaboration here. Some aspects will be dealt with later. The important point is that human nature theory in its modern or even contemporary form is really little different from what it was three hundred years ago.

Throughout Western history, those who have tried to fathom the mystery of their own species' complexity or uniqueness have asked a number of questions: Are human beings the sum total of what they appear to be, or are they something more? Are they masters of all they survey, or only the instrument of some unknown or semi-known force? Are they the result of a situation which they find themselves born into and nurtured through, and if so, can they transcend that situation or environment? And throughout this history, learned opinion has been eager to supply a variety of answers to these and other queries.

The contradictory claims as to the truth of what we are, ought to do, and can become are genuinely exasperating to anyone who compares them. Since they all cannot be correct, there is a temptation to reject them all as wrong, or only partially right. It is enough to make one an agnostic, not just in the religious sense but with regard to the truth of any general theory of human nature. In the face of this doubt, why do we still seek to erect general theories and demand that they be true? I think the only answer is that which I offered earlier: Whatever else we may be, we are truth-seeking creatures, and this characteristic sustains us in what constantly seems to be a fruitless quest.

With all of the inconsistencies and apparent inadequacies of previous theories, one characteristic stands out: They all (with some minor exceptions) have been products of their authors' time and context. Their formulators tried to cast their analyses in the mold of their past and immediate experience. If Marx and Freud brought to bear dimensions of knowledge unknown to Plato or Augustine, this was as it should be; and if their analyses, in turn, seem inadequate to us today, that is to be expected. What this means is that contemporary human nature theorizing must be rooted in what we now know about ourselves, knowledge which far surpasses that of even our most recent predecessors.

Given the explosion of knowledge which has led so recently to an almost Faustian control of our environment and of ourselves—a knowledge which cannot be ignored but must be embraced—any attempt to generalize about the uniqueness of our species must consider this data in as great detail as possible. One danger, of course, is that one can easily become lost in the detail—there is so much, it is so complicated, and no one yet has succeeded in synthesizing it. Yet, the effort must be made. I repeat that no contemporary general theory of human nature can even begin unless full attention is paid to the findings of the natural sciences. Generally described "social theory" that excludes the natural sciences, and the life sciences in particular, is doomed from the start—it is as though one were writing a history of the wheeled vehicle and concluded the survey with the covered wagon.

Thus contemporary philosophers of human nature must accept anew the burden that has been bequeathed to them —to hypothesize and theorize about the real world to the fullest extent to which that world is now known. And, they must do so using the analytical tools of modern science. With such an effort, they may come after all to possess the "Philosopher's Stone."

II

The Philosopher's Stone

The science of human nature
is, like all other sciences,
reduced to a few clear points:
there are not many certain
truths in this world.

Alexander Pope
An Essay on Man — "The Design"

The book of Genesis relates a story of creation. Despite the symbolic phallic presence of the serpent, the sin of Adam and Eve was not sexual. Instead, their fault was hubris, an arrogant desire to know the secret of the Tree of Life, and with such a possession, to equal the power of their creator. For their presumption they were cursed and punished. Henceforth, they and their offspring were forced to toil for their daily bread, to suffer pain in childbirth and turmoil and disappointment through life. But worst of all, they now faced the ultimate travail of mortality—physical death.

Through this myth our ancestors sought to explain and reconcile the hard facts of their existence and the end of that existence as well. With a conjured realm of the fabulous they could make some sense of the never-ending cycles of birth and death, pleasure and pain, origins and ends.

We may dismiss the contents of this and other myths of our primitive forebears for what they were—grossly fanciful attempts to solve life's mysteries. What cannot be ignored, nor underestimated, is the effort itself, for that speaks volumes as to what we are. As a myth-making animal, the storyteller to future generations, we know ourselves as time-binding questioners. But with this perspective we are able to recognize the deficiencies and errors of previously accepted truths. Thus we possess a dual awareness: We know we are capable of inquiring profoundly about ourselves and all of nature, while at the same time we realize the uncertainty of the answers we provide. We are smug in abandoning the myths of the past, but uneasy in the realization that we may be constructing a new mythology for the future. Our myth-making capacity serves to remind us that not only is our knowledge of reality limited, but so too is our certainty of the knowledge we do possess. The medieval alchemists unsuccessfully sought the "Philosopher's Stone," the mythical agent elixir of life and immortality. We may have abandoned their specific quest, but that same urge to possess the truth haunts us still. Perhaps the real curse bequeathed to us as humans is the insatiable need to know, coupled with the awareness that we may never know with surety that what we know is true.

This obvious skepticism is inescapable and verified by our most mundane experiences. How often does our common sense affirm the truth of a matter, only to be doubted by an "inner sense" that requires us to stop and reconsider? On the grander scale of the physical sciences the rejection of the Ptolemaic theory of the universe is a case in point. Accepted for a millennium, it was set aside in a few generations by Copernicus, Bruno, and Galileo, some of whose own theories have been eclipsed in our century by those of Einstein. Given these and other regular assaults on our credulity, the only reasonable conclusion is that as human beings we are doomed to doubt. What becomes apparent is that genuine hubris is not the presumption to seek the truth, but rather the arrogant assumption of the dogmatist who claims to possess it. A healthy skepticism ought not to be viewed as a form of intellectual paralysis, but rather as a means to quarantine unwarranted pretensions to truth. In such a reference frame a study of ourselves can proceed without cant or embarrassment.

Even though severe restrictions on our ability to know with certainty must be conceded, it is still possible to reach valid conclusions about ourselves and our behavior. A sound epistemological base is a prerequisite and can be found in a modified (or expanded) empirical theory of knowledge. The brief sketch which follows will place my approach in perspective while clarifying at the outset a number of recurrent terms in my argument. The latter can be more fairly judged if these definitions are kept in mind.

Epistemology, the study of the nature and limits of human knowledge, has been an integral part of the Western philosophical tradition since its inception. In this subfield of philosophy two terms have been employed to describe two distinct ways of perceiving and verifying truth: *a priori* and *a posteriori*.

Plato, for example, held that human beings possessed innate ideas, an inborn knowledge of reality which was discoverable through life-long reflection.[5] His method of knowing was *a priori* in that he assumed certain principles to be self-evident, prior to experience, self-defining, undeniable. Such ideas or principles, rules or guides or even facts were viewed as existing in an absolute, infinite, unchanging form. If such ideas existed, they would do so in a certain, unqualified manner. At the core of Platonic thought was the assumption that this knowledge was real and was attainable by a select few, who could and should rule as philosopher kings.

A priori reasoning is deduction, beginning with a first principle and proceeding to a conclusion. If the first principle is undeniably true, and the statements which follow do so logically, then the conclusion must be true as well. Hence, if humans are indeed psychologically constructed as Plato presumed them to be, his conclusion, argued with impeccable logic, must be accepted. The problem, of course, is with the word "if." If Plato (or anyone else) were privy to an absolute truth, and if there were absolute truths in the first place, then all is well. But what "if" there are no absolute truths, or what "if" no one, not even Plato, can attain them?

The second term, *a posteriori*, refers to the process of induction. In such a procedure one reasons from observed effects or facts backward to a primary cause or general theory. Thus, if my observation and experimentation reveal that human beings, alone among organisms, possess a characteristic enlargement of the brain, I may reasonably conclude that an essential mark of humanity is the presence of a neo-cortex. The validity of my conclusion, however, may be questioned on two bases: Was my sample large enough, and was my vehicle of perception (my senses) trustworthy? Thus, the process of my reasoning may be perfect, but the material that I am reasoning about or with may be inadequate or in error.

Perhaps the earliest practitioner of this latter method was Aristotle. Unlike Plato, his mentor, he displayed an eclectic curiosity about all natural phenomena and concluded that, despite enormous dissimilarities, beings shared a common oneness with each other. Human beings, for example, might vary from each other in innumerable ways ("accidentally") but shared a fundamental form of existence ("substance") which distinguished them from all other beings. The wife, the lover, the son or daughter, the mother, father, or obnoxious neighbor, the king or freeman, though different from each other, were alike in the single respect of their humanity, and, as such, essentially different from the dog, the sparrow, or the rock. Observation and experimentation were thus crucial in ascertaining the truth about reality. Turning his attention to over 150 different political communities, Aristotle gleaned from this data a number of general principles which he concluded operated in them all, regardless of their obvious variety.

At the very genesis of the Western philosophical tradition we see exemplified two radically divergent approaches to the matters of human knowledge and truth, a divergence which still persists today. The Platonic (*a priori*) view begins with a presumed truth and deduces to a conclusion ("I know thus, therefore . . ."); the Aristotlean (*a posteriori*) accumulates facts and induces to discrete generalities ("I observe thus and thus, therefore . . ."). The former method has provided us with ideologies; the latter has equipped us with the scientific or empirical method.

One of the more carelessly used words in our vocabulary is "absolute." Precisely, it means "without exception or condition; pure; perfect; unlimited; unchanging; independent from anything else; whole or complete." Such a specific meaning requires its very sparing use as few of us, upon reflection, would wish to apply it within the normal range of our experience. As previously applied to describe Plato's epistemology, it is appropriate, as it is in the presumption of the ideologue's dogma; it is unacceptable in the language of science.

For purposes of my analysis I intend to distinguish "absolute" from "universal." The latter may be defined as containing the notion of generality, as in "generally valid," or "generally present," corresponding to normal or usual expectation. Thus, a universally valid principle is one that generally applies, but not necessarily without real or logical exception. If, for example, we say "Incest is universally prohibited in human societies," we mean that far and away most communities ban the relationship, though there are exceptions to this rule.

The direct opposite of absolute is "relative," that is, something specific to a particular context at a particular time, but subject to change. Hence, we may observe that marriage is a universal human institution, the specific form of it being relative to different societies at different times and under various circumstances. Thus, something may be both universal and relative; neither characteristic implies absoluteness.

Two more terms require a brief note, "objective" and "subjective." The former refers to a concrete, sensible (perceptible by the sense) object or fact, something outside of or exterior to the knowing subject, and not dependent on that subject for its existence. The dog is an objective fact since I can perceive it as an object; in addition, if it is barking, that too is fact. Both the existence of the dog and the fact of its barking are external to me, the subject, and would exist even if I did not see and hear the beast. On the other hand, when we describe something as subjective we mean simply that it has its source in a subject, that is, a knowing being which can evaluate and make judgments. If I say that yesterday was a "good" day, I mean that for me, everything went well—subjectively I have decided that according to my criteria yesterday was better than other days which I have experienced and which I might judge to be bad days by comparison. On the other hand, for my neighbor, the day may have been intolerable, one of the worst and more forgettable of his experience. The "day" itself was neither inherently good nor bad, but only is so in the opinion of the subjects. Thus judgments such as a good or bad smell or a pleasing or disturbing musical composition are subjective evaluations about objective things.

Finally, it is important to recall that a value, though *subjective* in its origin, becomes an *objective* fact. If I subjectively decide that yesterday was a good day for me then my *judgment* becomes an objective fact. If I am asked what kind of a day it was for me and I answer that it was "good," my questioner then concludes that it is a fact that I feel I had a good day. The day was not objectively good or bad itself, but my evaluation of it is an objective fact. With these definitions in mind it is easier to understand some historic attempts to explain how we know what we know and to what degree we can be certain that our knowledge is true.

René Descartes (1596–1650) is credited with the beginning of modern philosophy. He did not discover something totally new under the sun (or in the mind), but he did effect a break with a thousand-year-old tradition which had assumed a necessary link between theology and philosophy. What Descartes attempted was an unlinking of this often uneasy alliance and the founding of philosophy on "certain" truth. As a mathematician he not surprisingly felt that philosophy could be based on the same kind of first principles as geometry. This would eliminate the fuzziness and false assumptions which he felt had come to dominate philosophical thought. But first he had to face the problem of truth and the human mind's ability to discern it.

Descartes' metaphorical intellectual encounter with the evil genie of deception is a familiar story which needs no retelling here.[6] Suffice to recall that the impact of his famous treatise, *Discourse on Method*, has permeated all subsequent formal philosophy to this day. Of primary interest here is his emphasis on sense perception as the source of human knowledge, and his analytical method that was to become the *sine qua non* for modern natural and, in some respects, social science.

Descartes advised that all problems should be approached analytically in such a way as to reduce them first to their simplest ingredients, and then to proceed to a solution by minimal, incremental steps, each step carefully calculated so that it revealed only clear and distinct ideas. By the latter he meant ideas that were demonstrable, as in knowledge that could be shared and generally accepted at face value. As to the source of human knowledge about "nature" (i.e., existential reality), it lay in the human capacity of sense perception. But precisely because any or all of the senses could betray one, that is, be subject to error, the careful process of checking and cross-checking observable data was necessary. The net result was a notion that general knowledge could only be obtained and transmitted through the senses, which could barely be trusted, by means of a method of deduction, that is, by advancing from the general to the particular. The irony is that the empirical, scientific method of induction, moving from the particular to the general, owes so much to Descartes. The byways, backroads, and alleys that account for this reversal were not so important as the fact that Descartes laid the foundation for a confused theory of knowledge which would require centuries to sort out. Many even feel that formal philosophy has yet to win victory in this battle.

What Descartes' intellectual followers received from him was a modern reassertion that human beings come to knowledge by means of their senses, that one is not born with a full panoply of knowledge, like Platonic ideas that merely remain to be discovered. Lurking within this assumption, however, was the genie of doubt, the fallibility of those self-same senses. Presumably, careful deduction from empirically induced generalities could save the day, and certain truth be revealed. But herein lay a trap into which John Locke was to blithely stumble.

Locke (1632–1704) in so many ways epitomizes Rationalist philosophy that his name may be forever synonymous with it. As an inheritor of Descartes' method Locke told his audience that man is born with a *tabula rasa*, a mind like a blank slate upon which nothing has been written. In other words, man is not born with *a priori*, innate ideas or knowledge. Whence comes man's knowledge then? As a good Cartesian, Locke says, through the senses, through experience.

In his *Second Treatise on Civil Government*, however, Locke states without qualification that human beings are born free, rational, social, and equal and because of this birthright, endowed with inalienable rights to life, liberty, and property. Though a majority of his audience applauded this rhetoric, largely because it echoed their own bias against the presumptions to authoritarian rule by the Stuart kings, it required another century before a cooler head could chronicle the logical inconsistencies in Locke's statements.

That cool, even frosty, intellect emerged in the eighteenth century in the person of David Hume (1711-1776). His critique of decadent Rationalist philosophy is still unsurpassed, as is the framework for modern epistemology which he provided. He singlehandedly reduced to intellectual ashes the presumptions and contradictions of his Rationalist predecessors in philosophy, while simultaneously challenging the arrogant confidence of his contemporaries in the natural sciences. All of this he accomplished quietly through a life of independent study. Yet perhaps no writer until our time has done so much to clear the air for human nature theory. If we are better able today to understand the limits of our knowledge it is because of the analysis of this gentle Scot.[7]

What Hume perceived as inconsistent in Locke's various arguments was the latter's initial acceptance of the empirical theory of knowledge—all knowing is the result of sense experience, not *a prioris*—and his later bald rhetoric declaiming some original or natural human characteristics, from which some kind of natural rights could be logically derived. The obvious query today, in reading Locke's works—but little noted until Hume—is: How can Locke on the one hand deny *a priori* knowledge and then later implicitly affirm on just such a basis a description of the natural, pre-political person? When Locke affirms, without blush or disclaimer, that humans are born free, equal, rational, and social, these are descriptions which require proof of consensual agreement on the terms' definitions as well as proof of the existential human conditions described. But Locke does not feel compelled to provide such proof. He asks his readers to accept these statements as givens, self-definitions—in effect, *a prioris*.[8] We may not have needed Hume to reveal this contradiction to us, but it certainly has been to our advantage to have his critique.

Hume's analysis of Rationalist epistemology may be summarized as his attempt to disentangle three skeins which had been confusedly woven together. He referred to them as the misuse of the term "Reason," which had become by his time a catch-all concept that included virtually anything which the Rationalists wished to discuss or prove. To correct this he proposed arguments which are critical to my inquiry and can be summarized as follows.

Hume's analysis may be described as a triad. He contended that knowledge and its truth derivatives (or verifiability) involve three levels, the first of which is the mathematical proposition. For example, *if* A = B, and *if* B = C, then A = C. The essential element in this proposition is the conditional "if." No knowledge of the factors' relationship to reality is necessary; the factors are symbols, constructs of the mind; their individual verifiability is extraneous to the truth-value of the proposition. The "truth" of the proposition's conclusion (A = C) lies in the *relationship* between the conditional propositions. The conclusion is "absolute truth," in the sense that the mind cannot logically conceive of an alternative or contradiction to the conclusion. This is Hume's "litmus test," a test which only mathematical knowledge can pass.

The second category of truth lies in "fact." The material involved here is concrete, objective reality. Since the Rationalists, following Descartes, had rejected as a source of truth *a priori*, innate ideas, knowledge had become a sensory derivative—the mind comes to knowledge through the senses. Hume said that such knowledge can yield only probable truth since, by definition, its source is sensory and as such potentially in error. Since the senses can deceive, knowledge derived from them cannot be presumed to be infallible or absolutely true. This does not mean that this knowledge is necessarily inaccurate, only that it cannot logically be asserted without doubt. What the mind asserts as fact, therefore, is an impression of reality, and no matter how widely held by how many minds, it remains subject to the test of absolute incontravertability, a test which it cannot logically pass. Knowledge derived from the senses, therefore, can only be *probably* true.

Finally, the realm of value assertion is, according to Hume, precisely that, assertion. That a thing or a person possesses a quality (rectitude, beauty, justice) is purely a subjective determination of the viewer or subject. It is a matter of the preference of the viewer and, as such, has its source in "emotion" (for example, my previous "good" day).

It is irrelevant to detail subsequent attempts to cope with Hume's critique: They have either failed (Kant) or have circumvented the problem which he raised (Hegel *et al*). A metaphysical approach to the problem of knowledge such as Hegel's may be a valid alternative, but it is one which does not address itself to the necessity of examining human nature through the observable data of that nature's existence and behavior. Hume forces us to observe and to be skeptical of what we conclude from our observations.

Hume's analysis called into question that most sacred of scientific cows, the notion of cause and effect. Let us picture a scientist who feeds "x" amount of poison to ninety-nine mice, after which they all die. The "obvious" conclusion is that the poison has killed the mice. But the obvious, work-a-day common sense conclusion is not necessarily true, in the strict, logical sense. Logically, such a cause and effect relationship is only possible if one possesses absolutely certain knowledge of the essence of the elements involved and has taken into account all possible variables. This, of course, is physically impossible as it is beyond the capacity of empirical investigation and verification.

An empirical theory of knowledge relies on what can be observed. A soul, an essence, an *urstuff*, or nature cannot be measured, weighed, or examined. It may exist, but it cannot be quantified or catalogued. What exists is that which can be verified by the senses. To see and taste, smell and feel and hear—these are the means by which we self-described knowing animals come to knowledge. What Hume said, therefore, to the natural scientists of his time was that cause and effect may exist, but it cannot be logically proven; all that can be demonstrated is a sequence of events. For example, if water vaporizes over heat at 100^0 C, has the heat *caused* the change? Perhaps so—but perhaps no. Logically something else may have caused it. Not surprisingly, the natural scientists of his day were nonplused by Hume's critical skepticism. If there was one thing which these scholars were certain of, it was the absolute truth of their conclusions, based as they supposedly were on discovered, incontrovertible, universal principles. But their truths were derivable from sense-perceived data or experience. As such, according to Hume's logic, this knowledge and its derived conclusions, might be true—but then again, it might not be.

The group most devastated by Hume's analysis, however, were the moral philosophers. His separation of fact from value, of what we would term today as the separation of the objective from the subjective, meant that all human values or judgments about quality must be considered relative to time, place, and circumstance—or in Hume's parlance "convention." Goodness, badness, beauty, justice could not be seen as inherent qualities of things, innate characteristics which could be discovered, but rather attributes awarded to objects by those objects' subjective observers. Hume was challenging the existence of absolute qualities, of standards of ethical behavior rooted in some sort of transcendental existence, of ideal truths or rules to be approximated or attained to. No longer could ethical philosophers refer to concepts such as inherent goodness or absolute justice with confidence of logical acceptance. These value-laden terms would have to be recognized for the subjective opinions which they were.

Hume was not destroying ethics, as many of his critics contended. He was providing a great service to ethical thought by cleansing normative speculation of its previous false reliances or presumptions. If properly viewed, he placed the art (or science) of human evaluation on a more honest, less arrogant basis—what we would call today, a non-ideological foundation.

Hume's critique could not be ignored nor was it. He synthesized and criticized the prevailing philosophy of his time in such a thorough manner that no one who approached the questions of truth and certainty could dismiss his analysis. He left us a number of options and consequences: (1) If we concede that all of human knowledge is the result of sensed experience, then we must admit the possibility that our knowledge might be in error. (2) As such, even the "hard" evidences of the natural sciences cannot be asserted as though either they or the conclusions derived from them are irrefutably certain—Hume's litmus test of the logical possibility, no matter how remote, of contradictions or alternatives, forces investigators to assert only the probability of their conclusions' truth. (3) In the matter of values, one must concede their relativity and subjective origins—that they are held or adhered to is an objective fact, but they remain the construct of the persons who construct them and therefore have even less claim to being demonstrably true than conclusions based on empirical evidence. This does not mean that there is no absolute standard or set of moral principles; it does mean that if such do exist, they cannot be proven empirically. This, in turn, does not mean that there is no universal (though ultimately still relative) set of moral standards, for there may be norms which, while subjective in their origin are so widely held that they are the common moral fund of all or nearly all human societies.[9]

I stated earlier that epistemology, as arid and abstract as it may appear, is crucial as a starting point for any discussion of human nature. We simply must have an acceptable basis for determining whether or not what we say is true, or at least to what degree it is so. Nowhere is this more evident than in the legacy of Hume. He leaves us with uncertainty (or at least only high degrees of probability) in the realm of natural science, but also with extreme concern as to whether our individual moral choices have any relevance beyond our own opinion. If this were not enough to make us uneasy, he forces us to consider the relativity of communal value systems, or what I will later call and define as "public moralities." Moral relativity at the communal level means that the norms or values of a society (and their resulting institutions) will vary according to the perceived needs and desires of a society at a given time and under particular circumstances. In this line of thinking, standards of justice, beauty, goodness, excellence and so forth are in the minds of the beholders, subject to change even within communities, and identifiable with other societies' value systems only by coincidental extension. If the phrase "Different strokes for different folks" has any significance it does so in this instance. I must stress again, however, that Hume's skepticism is purifying. It forces one to use care and precision in one's own thought and statements while reserving too ready acceptance of what others claim to be true. In short, it provides a perfect intellectual defense mechanism against the ideologue.

This in no respect means that the search for truth is a futile quest, nor that we must accept moral relativity to the point of anarchy. On the contrary, as the natural sciences daily demonstrate, probable (as opposed to logically "absolute") truth is perfectly compatible with scientific inquiry and conclusions, while, as I hope to demonstrate, human normative systems and beliefs can be shown to possess a primary, empirical base which underlies their secondary, subjective articulations. Ironically, Hume's skepticism will prove to be the catalyst for the discovery of a scientific basis for human morality. This is the conclusion which the following discussion should reveal.

If one thing piques a scientist's curiosity, it is recurrence or pattern. When the same disease symptoms recur, a pathologist will hypothesize that there may be a single cause. So, too, when human interaction repeats itself, the student of that behavior should likewise question if the repetition is due to a common cause. All of the oral and written history of our species records recurring patterns of love, hate, fear, competition, greed, aggression, and many more emotions and reactions. So too, we have chronicled the institutions which either ratify, limit, or extend these responses. Marriage and sport, war and trade, law and politics and religion—all are, if anything, the institutional means which humans have used to perpetuate, forestall, or enhance their existence—or so it would seem from a view of our past. If there are constants in the physical environment which the physicist can point to as at least highly probable benchmarks or rules, why should the consistency of human behavior and institutions not be accorded the same status? The claim seems appropriate that the history of our species is a picture of ourselves as we are. The picture may be at times blurred, even abstract, but it is not impenetrable. In this respect I propose to seek our information about ourselves by examining what we know from our past and can easily agree upon. My suspicion is that if our past is not yet our prologue, it is at least consistent with our present—the way we are.

In this inquiry I will also be concerned with many facts that have come to light in the past few decades which give us a much more profound understanding of our organic complexity. I will try to follow Descartes' exhortation of reducing problems to their simplest components and advancing step by step with conclusions which can be clearly accepted. In doing so, however, I am at risk of being accused of "reductionism," and may as well anticipate this charge now.

It has been fashionable in philosophical circles to criticize attempts at synthesis as "reductionist." The fault of the synthesizer, according to the critics, is that by seeking a better understanding of a complex whole through a closer examination of its parts, the synthesizer oversimplifies. The oversimplification automatically represents a distortion, a "reduction" of the complex to the simple, a loss of appreciation of the whole in favor of the parts. Most deplorable in many critics' eyes is any effort to explain varied and multiple human behavior in terms of its physical components. The horror of such an investigation is that it must perforce assume that human nature may be more thoroughly understood through its biology. Hence, humans are supposedly diminished by even the suspicion that their behavior could, for example, be predisposed. Presumably, also there is no room left to consider humanity in its spiritual dimensions.

Leaving aside temporarily the fact that the "fact" of this spiritual dimension of human nature has never been demonstrated and hence still remains at the level of unfounded assumption, this critique in its various forms involves a number of errors. It gratuitously assumes that human nature is so essentially distinct from other living organisms that any but the most superficial comparison with them or their parts must be false. Such an assumption itself requires proof that has never been forthcoming; indeed, the opposite is more obvious and logically compelling, namely, that as a proven part of an organic continuum, we as humans share with other life forms more that is common than is distinct.

Next, attributes assigned to ourselves, by ourselves, are not necessarily true. We may depict ourselves any way we wish—as fundamentally cooperative and social (Locke), as basically selfish and aggressive (Hobbes), as driven by economic motivation (Marx), as trifurcated and forever naturally unequal (Plato), or as ruled by a rational, absolute, and demanding creator (Augustine). These authors, among others, have offered views of human nature which either purport to be *a priori*, but are not, or are empirically based, but only incompletely so. In both instances several observed or wished for characteristics or phenomena have been isolated, then elevated to a generalization of the entire organism. Hence, there is at work a kind of reductionism in reverse. Instead of a complex whole reduced to simpler form, a part or parts are exaggerated and identified as the whole. Who, for example, can reasonably disagree with numerous particular insights of Marx or Hobbes? Once said, however, their ultimate generalizations strike us as forced and truncated versions of the human reality.[10]

To examine the composition of our human elements and their interactions through integration, so as to better understand the totality of the creature, is the only rigorous way to proceed to a more complete understanding of ourselves. We alone among the animals possess the ability to understand what we sense, to make a judgment on the accuracy of our perceptions, and to choose to act in terms of those judgments to achieve an end. A truly holistic understanding of ourselves must begin with a hypothesis that, though the whole may be greater than its parts, the former cannot be understood, much less appreciated, unless the latter are as well. I cannot concede that such an approach is oversimplification, but rather prefer to argue that it is the only proper way to proceed to an eventual fuller understanding of human nature.

III

In Search of the Beast

Go, wondrous creature! mount where
    science guides
Go, measure earth, weigh air, and
    state the tides;
Instruct the planets in what orbs
    to run,
Correct old time, and regulate
    the sun

                Alexander Pope
              An Essay on Man

One of our more popular contemporary clichés is the word
"revolutionary." The original social and political meaning
of the term is now supplemented by reference to any kind
of upheaval taking place in the arts, sciences, and technology—everything from the latest fad in women's fashion,
to a new automobile tire, to lunar landings is touted as not
just new, but revolutionary.

Diluted in meaning by misuse and overuse as it might
be, it remains the only adequate term to describe recent
advances in the biological and related life sciences. The list
of scientific journals representing new sub-fields carries
names which are scarcely comprehensible to even the most
liberally educated laymen. Microbiology, paleoanthropology, ethology, mathematical genetics—to name but a
few, and then only those related to the life sciences—are
disciplines which have extended and deepened our knowledge of living beings. Similar extensions have occurred in
the fields of physics, chemistry, and astronomy.

At first glance this seeming proliferation of scientific

disciplines gives the impression of rampant specification—of knowing or discovering more and more about less and less. Quite the opposite is true, for what were once considered discrete boundaries among sciences—say, biology, chemistry, and physics—have disappeared or are rapidly doing so. These three traditional prime sciences now overlap, impinge upon each other, and increasingly reenforce each other's findings and techniques. There would be no viable, verifiable science of ancient human beginnings, paleoanthropology, without carbon and potassium isotope dating techniques, geological stratology, cytology, and many more -ologies from scientific endeavors previously presumed unrelated. By the same token, as the lines between the sciences have blurred, the gulf between the natural and social sciences has narrowed. It is no longer possible to fruitfully enquire about the process or content of human knowledge, for example, in ignorance of the organic seat of that knowledge—the human brain. Our knowledge of ourselves and of our world has not only expanded geometrically but has taken a synthetic turn—a recognition of the enormous interdependency of all organic and nonorganic existence. How much different is this view from that portrayed in the first two books of the Old Testament, where in Genesis we are told of the sequential and separate creation of the universe and creatures therein? Strangely enough the myth does imply a notion of continuity, of ascendancy and descendancy, of the unity within matter which we have now come to accept and take for granted. But if God is considered by some to be the father of Adam and Eve then the title of godfather of our modern view of ourselves must be given to Charles Darwin.[11]

Yahweh required only six days for his creative work, but Darwin needed over twenty years to produce *On the Origin of the Species.* After years of observation, travel, thought, and procrastination, Darwin outlined his theory that all living species—indeed, by implication, all species—share a commonality, and that higher (that is, more complex) species derive over enormous periods of time from more or less common ancestors. From these common sources there derived specification, a development of many from one. And the key to it all is what Darwin called "natural selection." Natural selection, in Darwin's terms, meant that the more successful an organism was in its performance within its environment, the more likely it was to reproduce and the more likely that its characteristics would be passed on. It should be noted that terms such as "evolution" and "success" in reference to species must not be understood in any qualitative sense. Darwin himself rarely used the former term to avoid the implication that it connoted "progress."

The notion of the evolution of living beings was not original with Darwin. From Empedocles and Aristotle in ancient Greece, through Bacon to Lemarck and the poet Goethe, the idea gained increasing acceptance. Darwin's own contemporary, A. R. Wallace, had arrived at the same conclusion independently, and at the same time. But it was Darwin's publication and name which set the tone for a confrontation of the new science with the old beliefs, a confrontation, which in some quarters, still persists.

The theory of organic evolution through natural selection has undergone a number of important modifications in the one hundred years since it was formally proposed by Darwin. Despite (or better, because of) these refinements the hypothesis stands vindicated, the hysterical attacks of religious fundamentalists notwithstanding.

Darwin's original thesis came to be called "gradualism" on the basis of his proposal that organic development took place over uncounted millions of years. A problem with this view then, and to a certain extent still, is the lack of fossil evidence between species which would verify the development of one species from another. Of course soft-bodied organisms could not and cannot fossilize; this phenomenon can only occur when a hard substance such as bone or wood is pressurized and gradually replaced by limestone. But what of skeletal organisms whose fossil remains are nearly identical to those of their modern successors, as with some mollusks and insects? In these cases, millions of years of existence have witnessed no substantial change in the organisms at all. On the other hand, the only example of a definite traceable fossil linkage from an earlier form has long been the horse. In short, the lack of transitional fossil evidence in species where it could be expected to occur cast doubt on the notion of species linkage, as did the very lack of change in many species over enormous time spans.

Darwin recognized and admitted this difficulty but maintained that the fossil record, though imperfect, would eventually become more complete. In many respects his faith has been rewarded, but not sufficiently to satisfy some skeptics. Still another problem has arisen in recent years due to more accurate means of estimating time spans. Even if our solar system is roughly four and a half billion years old, there would not have elapsed enough time to allow for the intricate evolution of species which a gradualist theory would require.

Some evolutionists adopted the alternative view of "saltationism" (from the Latin *saltare*—to leap). In this view both the problems of missing fossil evidence and insufficient time were solved by positing a series of rapid jumps or leaps occurring very quickly, followed by long periods of stasis during which little or no change took place. Such a view would account for the seeming singularity or separateness among species and allow for evolution taking place in a more compressed time frame. Early geneticists favored this view. Finally in the 1930s a synthesis of the two views was proposed by Julian Huxley, grandson of Darwin's great defender, T. H. Huxley. The synthesis, to which I will return shortly, was largely the result of geneticists' increasing awareness of the fact that hereditary traits are the result of many genes working in combination. In the 1970s the debate resurfaced and has spawned a new interest in saltationist theory under the name of "punctuated equilibrium."[12]

Darwin, of course, knew nothing of genetics, for it is a science of our century. Few if any sciences have advanced so swiftly or elegantly as has genetics. If a single founder can be named it must be the nineteenth-century Austrian monk, Gregor Mendel. His experiments in crossbreeding peas led him to postulate the existence of inherited characteristics which would regularly recur generation after generation or reappear after seemingly disappearing—the result of what we now call dominant and recessive genes. His studies made no impact during his lifetime and it was only early in this century, upon the rediscovery of his papers, that genetics as a separate discipline was born. Researchers located these factors of heredity on the chromosomes of the cell nucleus. Though they could predict with near mathematical certainty the results of cross-breeding and inbreeding, the secret of what these genes actually were eluded them. The puzzle was finally solved in 1953 with the model of the double helix configuration of the deoxyribonucleic acid molecule (DNA) described by James D. Watson and Francis Crick.[13] Since 1944 DNA had been the suspected chemical transmitter of genetic information, but Watson and Crick accurately defined the structure (the double spiral) of its content (the four chemical units of adenine, guanine, cytosine, and thymine), thus setting off a virtual explosion of knowledge within the field of genetics. In less than thirty years scientists and technicians have moved from this singular discovery to methods of splicing and recombining this substance, to its artificial manufacture, to the legal patenting and wholesale production of brand new organisms. Without exaggeration, we can now claim knowledge of life itself, at least at the cellular level, and have the ability to create new forms of life while altering existing forms. Perhaps the search for the Philosopher's Stone has actually ended at last.

But if we now know infinitely more about the essence of life itself, we have also gained immeasurable insight into our human evolutionary past. Fossilized remains of our purported pre-human ancestors were unearthed in the last years of the nineteenth century, but it is only since the 1920s that a true science of paleoanthropology has itself evolved. If Mendel conceived genetics, then the new science of pre- and early man was nurtured by Raymond A. Dart, a South African professor of anatomy at the University of Witwatersrand in Johannesburg. In 1924 Dart received from a colleague a fossilized skull which he was to describe as a child, neither ape nor human, but with some very humanlike characteristics. The Taung skull, named from the limeworks where it was found, had belonged to a creature that had hominid dentition, stood at least semi-erect, and was bipedal. Its brain was quite small by our modern standards, but it was definitely not an ape. Though rejected for over a quarter of a century by the scientific establishment, Dart's claim to have found an indirect precursor of *Homo sapiens* is now accepted. The name he gave the creature, *Australopithecus africanus*, has passed into our general vocabulary, and the study of human origins has itself taken a giant leap in the past fifty years.[14]

The Taung skull has been dated at between two and three million years old. As dating techniques have improved, and the number of fossil discoveries has increased in the past thirty years, Darwin's optimistic prediction has partially come true: The gaps are being filled in and much more rapidly than might have been expected. New names and age dates have been added to the old list of Cro-Magnon, Neanderthal, and Java Man. These now include: *Homo erectus* (.4 to 1.6 million), *Homo habilis* (1.6 to 2.2), and *Australopithecus afarensis* (2.8 to 3.8). As new fossil finds almost tumble upon each other, stronger links are added in the chain which binds us to creatures who inhabited Africa many millions of years ago. That these (and most likely others yet to be discovered) were among our forebears can no longer reasonably be denied. Many questions still remain, perhaps the most fascinating being "How did these early hominids live?" Again we may probably never have enough answers but we can surmise a great deal from the fossil sites. For example, it seems evident that *H. erectus* (Peking Man) possessed the controlled use of fire while his earlier relative, *H. habilis*, with a brain size fully thirty per-cent smaller than ours, nevertheless made and used crude stone tools (and probably weapons). The life-style implica-tions of these and other facts of their physical existence are many but at least include the phenomena of cooperation, communal living, meat-eating and intraspecific, lethal aggression—and all of this before the acquisition of our modern "big-brain." In other words, our expanded cerebral capacity did not precede, and therefore account for, our abilities to do so many things which until now we have considered distinctly human qualities. We walked upright, made tools, shaped our environment, fought and loved one another millions of years ago—all with a brain no larger than that of a modern ape's.

Though many supporting sciences and sub-fields have contributed to our contemporary knowledge of ourselves (for example, geology in many of its forms) the major impact on contemporary human nature theory has come from modern genetics and paleoanthropology. Combined or mutually supportive, they have verified that modern humans are the product of evolutionary development in particular, and are part of an equally verifiable evolution of all organic matter in general. Whether differentiation among species is the result of "gradualism" or the vaults and halts of "punctuated equilibrium," or a combination of both processes is no longer of crucial importance. What has been established, and increasingly verified by almost daily advances, is the unity of organic matter, a unity which lurks within living cells in the form of shared proteir.s, enzymes, and acids. As the life sciences are continually discovering their greater commonality with each other, we are recognizing the vast reservoir of similarity which all life shares.[15] This is as it must be, for our uniqueness as a species can only be fully appreciated after our sameness with other animals is discerned, just as our uniqueness as individuals within our own species is explicable only after our identity with our species is recognized. Appreciation of this bond with other creatures which squirm or fly, swim or leap in no way reduces or diminishes us. Our link in an organic chain, a phylogenetic continuum, is a reality that should serve to make us more appreciative of the complexity that we have achieved as a species. However, before we get carried away with a secular version of the pride of angels, that is, become too blasé over our luck in having reached our present plateau of evolution, we should first note some physical features of our being which are both puzzling, and in some cases, unique to us.

The most obvious and special feature about *Homo sapiens* is our big brain, an organ proportionately larger and enormously more complex than its counterparts among

other animal species. Though we are far from a full understanding of its function, that we know anything about it at
all speaks volumes about its capacity. Other animals have
large and complicated nervous and cognitive centers which,
in the case of apes, whales, and dolphins, enable them to
communicate orally and store experiences as memory. But
only the human brain can turn upon itself to speculate as
to what it is. This reflective ability is unique to human
beings. Our brain is so special and so grand, so complete
and self-contained that it can do that which the ancients
ascribed as a singular power of God—contemplate itself! If
a contemporary candidate for the seat of the soul were
offered, the human brain would have no competition.

This gelatinous mass of roughly a trillion cells remains
largely a mystery to itself—but it is gaining ground rapidly.
It now knows its chemical composition, its organic sub-
parts, and much of what it calls its interactive functions. It
is partially aware of when, how, and why some of its components misfunction and how to restore a disrupted order.
The brain can partially describe itself and its relationship
to the rest of its biological vessel but in all these areas it is
still child-like—groping, hesitant, and immature. With its
record to date, however, the odds are in its favor that it
will not cease until it finally knows itself in its fullness.
Will it then, as perhaps it should, call itself god?[16]

The human brain knows that it shares some of its parts
with many other creatures. The now generally accepted
description of this organ is the "triune brain," a single
organ with three distinctive, though interfunctional parts.

The primary segment is the so-called "reptilian brain."
Consisting of the spinal stem and a nodular terminus, the
medulla oblongata, it is the possession, in some form, of all
vertebrates, and in many, the only brain they have. Regu-
lating everything from peristalsis—the intake of food to
waste removal—to lung action and heart beat, the medulla
is the source of movement control and is referred to by its
more sophisticated sibling as the primitive brain. This
"unwitting one" originates instinctive behavior.

The cerebrum atop the medulla is also a brain part that
in humans is shared with other animals, and is dubbed the

"old mammalian brain." Larger, denser with cells and synapses, this part of the organ is the limbic system, which functions in concert with its more primitive relative to give emotional coloration to instinctive activity.

The third set of circuits, the cerebellum or "new mammalian brain," is a deeply wrinkled, convoluted mass of grayish tissue which, from a biological standpoint, is that which makes man what he is as a separate species. In its complex functioning—an interaction of specialized cell systems—it is both the source and the location of memory, conceptualization, and verbal expression—the physical seat of what we call thought, and the means by which it is expressed.

Our brain has learned a great deal about itself in a very short time concerning the degree to which its three parts function together or separately, the interconnecting circuitry of various parts or locations, and the effects of hormones and drugs on this complex circuitry.

This brief description of our most distinctive biological feature would be incomplete if the most special product of that unique equipment were not noted—language. Not only are we capable of producing concepts or ideas—notions of what is, was, and will be—but we can communicate or transmit these phenomena to other members of our species. The transmission may be simple at one extreme, tediously complex at the other, and, in most instances, somewhere in between. The result is, nevertheless, a forest of knowledge, sometimes permanently and elaborately recorded, and certainly unique to us. This very communication between author and reader is example enough of the human ability to defy space and mood, time and sequence to convey to each other those ideas, memories, and judgments which we feel are important. So remarkable is lingual ability that it may be recorded as our premier attribute. The title "tool-maker" no longer impresses us for its exclusivity—not when insects and birds and apes literally fashion and employ tools to achieve food or protection. Language, both oral and transcribed, is the mark of our beast, and its root is in our big brain. That organ has yet to fathom all of the physical factors that account for its wonderful ability, but at least it knows that it is wondrous.[17] Aristotle named us a political animal, who communicates complexly; for him, as we shall see, the two factors—humanity and lingual ablity—were in effect two sides of the same coin, both, the cause and effect of each other.

Perhaps one of the most startling, and in some ways disturbing, recent discoveries is the fact that male and female brains differ in structure and that this difference is due to the differentiated sex hormones. It may seem unnecessary to remind ourselves that the sexes are biologically different. But the folk wisdom that has always "known" that men and women think and act differently, in terms of different priorities—a folk wisdom so commonly scoffed at as myth —now enjoys the status of scientific truth. The evidence is already too convincing not to be accepted: The sex hormones, as they affect the hypothalmus gland deep in the brain, produce different synaptic densities, which in turn produce various behavior patterns or similar patterns in differing degrees. I will return to this extremely important fact when I discuss the biological bases of human behavior traits and their subsequent value structures.[18]

While noting this sexually related phenomenon we also ought to recall sexuality itself as both a product of and a spur to our evolutionary status. Reproduction, and hence perpetuation of the species, in our and many other species is the result of a cooperative effort on the part of two individuals who alone could not biologically achieve it. Why we are sexual is not of concern here; the point is that we are, and many other leapers, flyers, and swimmers with whom we live are as well. Among its many ramifications, sexuality means individuation, and paradoxically, with individuality is born death. The asexually reproducing or parthenogenic amoeba, continually dividing itself, never really perishes. The product of sexual reproduction, however, is genetically unique and, though a fixed proportion of its genes persist in a mathematically decreasing number in succeeding generations of its offspring, its own uniqueness ceases at its death. Is it surprising that a creature that knows itself as well as we do, which can speculate on its own mortality, should invent visions of immortality and seek means to escape this mortal coil?

We are aware of the fact that our brain is proportionately larger than other animals' and of the effects which that increased capacity and complexity produce. But why our primary and secondary sexual apparatuses should be of an equally disproportionate size is puzzling. The relative size of the male genitalia and the female breast appear to be overkill for their designated purposes of impregnation and nurturing. In addition, the human female seems unique among mammals with a neurologically rich genital tissue cluster whose sole purpose appears to be related to orgasm. This too seems superfluous for procreative inducement when hormonally regulated cycles in other mammals provide sufficient excitation to achieve this end. These and many other anomalies are not just curiosities but distinctive evolutionary features. If natural selection means breeding for success, (that is, successful breeding *and* nurturing of offspring to sexual maturity), then the assumption must be made that these features probably did and still do serve a purpose in the struggle for existence.[19]

In this vein is another of our singular characteristics, bipedalism. Though some apes may "walk" for short distances, only we have adopted an upright posture, freeing our hands to use our remarkable opposable thumbs, with which we can make and use the most intricate variety of tools. I do not mean to imply in this observation a cause and effect relationship or even a sequential development of these features, but merely to remind us of their connection. Surely our ability to intricately create and maneuver would be impossible without our manual dexterity, but at what point that dexterity evolved and what "caused" its development may never be positively known. We are quite certain that our ancestors were bipedal as much as nine million years ago and that this posture freed their hands for activities other than locomotion. But whether they were already manually dexterous before they walked upright is unknown. We know that as a species we are, and have been for a very long time, capable of doing a vast array of things which our non-bipedal animal brethren could not and cannot do. And finally we know that as important as our brain is in this whole interconnection of activity, our ancestors were nonetheless bipedal before that organ achieved anywhere near its present size.

Much speculation has centered around whether or to what extent our hominid forebears were meat-eaters. The controversy is far from academic for large-scale meat consumption necessitates hunting and killing, which in turn involves some degree of social organization and cooperation as well as the use of weapons to kill prey larger and quicker than our ancestors were. The killing of prey and protection of that kill from other predators could not have been accomplished in a haphazard manner. Bipedalism and manual dexterity would surely be requisite, as would the necessary dentition to rip and tear rather than munch and crunch. Finally, meat eating on a large scale, with its required killing, presupposes a degree of cunning and ferocity not necessarily always directed outside of the species: There exists some evidence that our pre-human ancestors not only killed their kind but dined on them as well.

Contrary to the "hunting hypothesis" is the view that pre- and early *Homo* roamed the African savannah as a gatherer of roots and fruits, supplementing its diet with small game, and scavenging the remains left by the great predators with whom it shared its habitat. The picture thus drawn is somewhat like that of the "seed eater" Indians of early California—a small, timid primitive, subsisting on the whims of an uncertain environment and fearfully competing with more ferocious scavengers than itself for the leftovers of even greater predators. While the image is not exactly glamorous, it does satisfy at least one romantic bias we seem intent on perpetuating as the true condition of our ancestors—the noble savage in a state of nature, doing its nonsanguine thing, in relative harmony with the rest of nature. It may have been so, but it is about as likely as Locke's metaphoric description of nature or eighteenth-century European depictions of beaded, laughing American Indian maidens.

There are a number of considerations that make this

extreme view of prehuman life and behavior most unlikely. The fossil evidence indicates a creature, which, though bipedal, was rather small, perhaps four feet tall at the most. As such, it could not compete successfully with large predators; indeed, it probably was itself their prey. Yet its teeth were not those of the herbivore, then or now, made for grinding large amounts of grass and plants. They were instead rather modern, representing the capacity to handle a variety of diets ranging from fruit and nuts to meat. It is logical to presume that all of these items were in its diet. But if its relatively small stature vis-à-vis other predators placed it at a disadvantage, it also precluded a meat diet gleaned exclusively from carrion. The African scavengers of today are no less tenacious than they were then, several million years ago. Only if armed and in a pack, could our creature have had success in a competition over a carcass. Let us suppose that our ancestors were armed and roved as a group sufficiently strong to drive off the hyenas and vultures of their day, could there have been enough leftovers to support this obviously proliferating species and all the other scavengers as well? Possible, of course, but not likely.

If their dentition allowed, as it seems to, a supplemental diet of fruits and nuts then these, in combination with scavenged meat, may have provided an adequate food supply. The problem is that it is a rare ecology which provides, then as now, at all seasons, edible and digestible fruits and roots. For the members of our emerging species in East Africa the environment was not radically different then from what it is now—a mixture of forest and savannah grasslands. Though the mixture and extent of each grew and receded over time, the general semi-aridity of the region prevailed. One thing is certain—neither the forests which they left nor the savannahs to which they gravitated, were orchards. Even in the South Seas, with a year round abundance of fruit, the populations have always benefitted from the fruit of the sea, their major source of protein—but this creature did not live near the sea, so its protein could not have come from that source.

Most likely our ancestors gathered what they could,

when they could, and scavenged in the same way. But given their population success, spreading east to Asia and north to the Middle East and Europe, a major source of their regular, predictable diet must have been meat—and they simply could not have scavenged enough. Pre- and emerging *Homo* must have been a hunter in its own right and an increasingly adept one at that.

British sailors are traditionally called "limeys," dating to the recognition in the eighteenth century that the disease scurvy was the result of a vitamin deficiency (later specifically identified as vitamin C), and that citrus fruit, rich in this vitamin, could prevent the malady. But Eskimos, never exposed to fresh fruit and vegetables in their diets, never suffered from scurvy. The reason is that these natives, until recent decades, ate large quantities of raw seal and walrus meat; in its uncooked form this meat is rich in vitamin C and only cooking destroys it.

Since the creature we are considering obviously did not lack for vitamin C, and since its farmer's market of fresh fruits and vegetables was only seasonal, and since it was millions of years away from the controlled use of fire by which it could cook indigestible plants and grains, it is most likely that meat was a very substantial part of its diet. How did it obtain the meat to nourish itself? Our ancestors must have hunted and killed. They were no doubt omnivores, but primarily carnivores.

To this view certain studies and arguments give further credence. The carnivore's digestive tract is unable to absorb and convert certain necessary fatty acids to useful form from a primary vegetable base. The human central nervous system is composed of fifty percent dry weight fatty acid. But the long-chained fatty acids, and certain structural fats, necessary for this system's development do not occur in simple form. Rather, they are converted by herbivores from the more basic linoleic and linolenic acids found in seeds and grass. When a carnivore consumes the muscle tissue of a herbivore, a further conversion takes place that produces the acids required for a bigger, more complex brain. In addition, since most primates cannot derive substantial nutriments from uncooked grain, grass, or leaves, and our species generally has controlled fire for cooking purposes for only 50,000 years while it has possessed the enlarged neocortex for at least 500,000 years, the strong possibility is that we have evolved from a primate line of increasingly heavy meat-eaters. By further extension it may be argued that without such consumption *Homo sapiens* would not have evolved at all.[20]

The jury is still out on this and many other aspects of our evolutionary past. The data which we have, however, points at least to an ancestor which somehow became upright, abandoning the trees of its earlier and primordial past; a creature which learned to run on two legs while throwing sticks and stones at its opponents; a smallish beast whose evolving teeth were dictating its diet (or perhaps, vice-versa); a little-brained mammal whose hand was changing, becoming more delicate and able to squeeze more gently; a creature with sex organs that more and more spoke of reproductive dominance in inhospitable circumstances. We were in process of becoming!

It must be stressed again that, at least to this point, it is impossible to definitely determine whether many of these abilities developed in sequence, and if so what the sequence was. Just as problematic is their developmental relationship to the enlarging brain—that is, which "caused" which, if indeed cause and effect were involved—or, as is more likely, an interdependency feedback (a fit and start and stop—a "punctuated equilibrium") was taking place. In one instance, however, a probable sequence must be considered, because the fossil evidence indicates it so strongly.

Since upright posture and manual dexterity can easily be seen as factors contributing to a primarily hunting and gathering way of life, and since these abilities preceded the dawn of our modern big brain, we very likely already possessed an array of what we now describe as "human qualities" before we achieved our present magnificent cranial organ. If this is the case, then that distinctive biological feature that accounts for our complex communicative abilities came after, and probably resulted from, our capacity to stand and run, to chip weapons and to throw them, and to live and hunt in a cooperative manner. If this is true, then much of what we recognize as human values and institutions, stemming from social intercourse, are not the result of our possession of a big brain but rather belonged to us long before that acquisition. And if this is true, sociality and politics, the latter tentatively defined here as the control of actual or potential intraspecies conflict, did not arise from conscious, big brain activity but rather preceded by eons the presence of the modern neocortex. In short we were already remarkable creatures before we could speak to each other in complex sentences. We were social and aggressive, loving and contentious, nurturing and abusive, creative and destructive—while sporting a brain a bit larger than a present-day chimpanzee. We were certainly not yet a political animal in the traditional definition of that term—but we were well on our way.

If there is a synthetic reason or cause for this phenomenon it is very likely to be found in that which lies between our thighs—the major biological elements of human sexuality.[21] I noted earlier the uniqueness of the human genitalia —the male's disproportionately large penis, relative to other species, and the female's clitoris, both organs suited to the provision of regular and intensive sexual gratification. Neither male organ size nor female organ sensitivity are directly related to procreation as such—a smaller penis could as easily provide impregnation, while female orgasm is unnecessary for conception. Human beings appear to be unique, therefore, in their ability to indulge in recreational as well as procreational sexual activity. Why? Given our success as a species, and the demands of natural selection, it is unlikely that these characteristics developed in a vacuum with no relation to reproductive success. Though physiologically these anomalies appear to be superfluous, it is difficult to believe that they are actually so. For a possible explanation, let us consider the notion of the "sex contract," a term which I have borrowed from anthropology, specifically from those writers who have recognized the inescapable link between human biology and behavior.[22]

A key factor in the evolution of any species is reproductive success, which includes the transference of survival-suitable biological characteristics to successive generations.

Such success is termed "fitness." Quite simply, maladaptive organisms will perish, sooner or later, while those which are adaptable, will survive, as will their offspring.

Alone among primate females, she of our species long ago transcended the limitation of estrus, or female heat, as the period of her sexual receptivity. Since her availability for, and one presumes, enjoyment of sex was not limited to her fertile period, she was capable of a sexual athleticism far in excess of the human male's capacity. The other side of the coin, however, was a definite vulnerability of her person during and after pregnancy, and the extreme vulnerability of her offspring through the long period to self-sufficiency. The sex contract theory reasonably proposes that these factors were mutually supporting and offsetting —the female was able to provide sex in quantity in exchange for the provision and protection that she and her children required. The most important consequence of this exchange for our ancestors would have been familial bonding, grouping of families, incipient social activity and institutions, greater and longer learning environments, and sustained personal protection—in short, all (or at least most) of the ingredients contributing to our present biological success.[23]

If we allow our perspective to range back millions of years, then this view of our species' origin is most compelling. Far more complex than presented here, the theory synthesizes the best data currently available from numerous cognate disciplines and provides more answers than not to many questions which have vexed human nature theorists, especially on the matter of respective role dominance of the sexes and the primary contribution of the female to the creation of the phenomenon of human bonding.

Contrary to the long-held view of human kinship originating as a male behavioral pattern, stemming from the close cooperation necessary in the primitive hunt, this theory focuses on the basic biological relationship between the female and her offspring. The more plausible picture that emerges is one of an increasingly sexually receptive and fecund female, requiring and retaining a greater amount of male protection and assistance for herself and her more numerous, later maturing offspring. From anonymous,

occasional sexual encounters, a kind of symbiotic relationship developed into what we would identify as a familial
bond, replete with mate identification, increasing male
constancy and exclusivity, and cooperation of both sexes
in the nurturing and rearing process. In this view the female
is seen as the matrix of the family in the truest sense of the
word, and as such the real nucleus and origin of future
human sociality.

The question of aggressiveness is another matter that has
concerned not only scientists but scholars and commenta-
tors in many fields in the past twenty years. Indeed, it is
fair to say that this has been one of the preoccupying issues
of human nature theorists since ancient times, and whole
social theories have been erected on the assumption that
we either are or are not naturally selfish and aggressive.
Since Locke, through Marx and to modern behavioral
psychology, the environmental thesis has prevailed, a presumption that aggression, and its sometimes lethal, violent
fall-out, is objective to us, that is, the result of an unsettled
violent environment and/or improper conditioning. So per-
vasive has this view been, especially among behavioral and
social scientists, that any challenge to its dogma has elicited
responses unmatched in their viciousness since Galileo suggested that the earth revolved around the sun. And perhaps
for similar reasons, since the guardians of the environmental thesis have much to lose if proven wrong.

The arguments of the antagonists and their relative
merits I have reserved for later extended discussion. Suffice
to note here that evolutionary and genetic theory and fact,
and the new study of animal behavior in its natural habitat,
ethology, have combined to provide a far more convincing
explanation of human aggression than anything forthcoming previously from pseudo- *a prioris* about fallen angels,
lost, happy states of nature, or Skinnerian boxes.

One key to the new, scientifically verifiable view of
human aggressivity has come from those animal behaviorists
who in the 1930s and 1940s concluded that animals whose
lives were spent behind bars in zoos were not necessarily
representative of their species in either health or behavior.

These biologists determined that an animal's "natural" behavior would only be apparent in their normal habitat. The pioneering work of Konrad Lorenz, Niko Tinbergen, and Karl von Frisch has been augmented and extended by Jane Goodall, Dian Fossey, and many others whose years of living with and carefully observing a vast array of animals breed, live, and die has enriched beyond measure our understanding and appreciation of our related fauna—and with it, ourselves.[24]

Before proceeding, two terms must be clearly defined and distinguished: *analogy*, by which is meant a likeness or similarity, and *homology*, which denotes an identity. In biology (as in literature, music, or architecture) there are two cardinal points or foci—substance and form. Distinction between living species can be described in these terms as well as can be a symphony or a novel. Thus, an ape, distinguishable from man by formal and substantial criteria (criteria, of course, which we have determined) performs a certain act, for example, suckling its infant. Other female mammals perform the same task with the same organic equipment for the same purpose. Though the species are different, the situation is homologous, the same, regardless of the different species. When the ape picks a particular twig or leaf and then uses this to extract termites for food, we conclude that this is *like* tool-making, an analogy or similarity to our own use of like objects for similar purposes. In common parlance we often refer to things as analogous ("his hair looks like a mop"), but we rarely use the word homologous, because we take for granted that when we are not using simile we intend to convey identity.

I point this out because it has become a bone of contention for critics of the ethological literature. When animal behavior is described in human terms it is often derided as anthropomorphism, as advancing a characteristic from the level of analogy to that of homology. The problem is that often times the distinction blurs and can become only a subjective judgment: When a dog and his human master urinate, the function can only be described as homologous; but if they both evidence relief after the act, is this only analogous?

With these distinctions, we can approach the work of the ethologists with greater discrimination especially in the case of animal aggression. The key which they have provided for this phenomenon is that aggression, to a greater or lesser degree, is typical in most vertebrate species, that in predator species it has two manifestations, and that in these species both of its forms serve a species-preserving function. That competition, much less aggression, should be thought beneficial to any species, including our own, has been enough to frighten many whose reputations and academic careers were built on a contrary premise.

The two modes or forms of aggression are now generally called *inter*specific and *intra*specific. The former refers to aggression between or among species, the typical prey-predator relationship in which the end sought is the death and consumption of the prey; the latter form of aggression is that which takes place within a species and ranges in degree of ferocity from competition, to fight display, to actual combat, and sometimes to the actual death of the contestants.

It is obvious that interspecies aggression and killing is a function of species preservation. We are all familiar with models of the food chain—how in ladder-fashion one species preys upon another and is itself the prey of yet another. Indeed, we have become much more aware of the intricacy of this chain and the ill effects that can result if one of the links is broken by the extinction of a single species. Even the destruction of a scavenger species—last in the food chain hierarchy—can disrupt an entire ecology as can the overkilling of a particular predator such as the coyote, the perennial bane of sheep raisers. Without the coyote to control the prairie dog population, one wonders if the latter, rather than the meek, would inherit the earth.

Not so obvious, however, is the beneficial effect of intra-species (or intraspecific) aggression. We might assume that the best, that is, most profitable, long-term effects for a species would be achieved through peace, harmony, and cooperation among its members, leading to reproductive success, and indeed, for many species this is the case. But for many others it is not. Reproductive success is, indeed, a requisite for a species' survival. For Darwin, as for modern biology, "fitness" is a measure of this reproductive success —those individuals within a species as well as those species best adapted to their environments will perpetuate their genes in a new generation. The qualities of behavior and physical characteristics best suited to this result within a given context will be most valuable in the long term. But this coincidence of contexts and characteristics may and does have different formulations for different species—there is no single pattern that applies to all organisms. Hence, strength, cunning, or agility may be factors conducive to reproductive success in some species, while being counterproductive for others. What Lorenz and other ethologists have quite adequately established is that, far from being universally destructive, forcefulness, competition, and even physical aggression are, for some species, necessary ingredients to guarantee their continued breeding success. In these species, this success will involve enticement of one, several, or many females, which in turn will be best facilitated through extreme competition, usually manifested by aggressive behavior on the part of contesting males. What the dominant male provides for his prospective mate is a territory, a specific ecological niche that is more suitable for rearing offspring than that afforded the loser. Given the odds, the better the location on a piece of coral reef, in a forest, or on a savannah, the greater the chances for the chiclid fish, the roe deer, or the baboon to see their offspring survive, prosper, and in their turn, reproduce.

To gain the best territory, thence to entice the best female, a male must aggressively defend his territory or dominant pack position against all other males which seek to displace him. He must fight. If he is a stag or a bull seal, he will take on all comers. The result is that those most adept in whatever techniques their species requires for reproduction will be successful. What the ethologists have found as a common pattern in animal behavior simply verifies Darwin's original insight—natural selection means reproductive success. What they added to that insight is the fact that intraspecific aggression is for some species the *sine qua non* that guarantees that reward.

Male aggressivity in the competition for breeding reward should not obscure the fact that this characteristic is innate in both sexes. The tenacity and ferocity displayed by females in defense of their offspring against both males and other females is well known and documented. The role of aggression in promoting reproductive success might better be pictured as a continuum of breeding-bearing-nurturing in which varying degrees of aggressive behavior are employed by both sexes at different stages in the process. This also points to the intimate connection between aggressivity and the whole panoply of behavior involved in the nurturing relationship between the female and her young. Thus, initial male aggressivity may be of benefit at the time of breeding but of less usefulness than nurturing qualities as time goes on.[25]

Lorenz's seminal thesis on animal aggression has been corroborated by two generations of subsequent scholarship, but with some major modifications. Most importantly, he observed that in those animal species that engaged in intra-specific aggression, (both in male versus male or female versus male or female), their violent activity most always ended short of the death of the weaker party, though occasionally severe wounding might prove accidentally fatal. He ascribed this "fail-safe" phenomenon to certain built-in mechanisms, reenforced by submissive rituals, which "automatically" prevented the stronger party from dealing the lethal blow. Thus, the defeated baboon male offering his buttocks for simulated copulation to his conqueror or the vanquished younger male wolf challenger extending his exposed neck to his dominant counterpart. The fight for dominance would be called off, submission made, wounds licked, hard feelings forgotten, and normalcy restored. From these and many other observations and data, Lorenz prematurely concluded that the human animal was the only one who regularly carried its aggressive, violent activity to the end—the death of the vanquished foe. He suggested that the reason for this difference lay in our brain. Refer-ring to the rather short period—one-half million years—in which the human brain nearly doubled in size, he specu-lated that it in effect out-distanced its internal "ritual

mechanisms," those stop-controls which appeared to be inherent in other animals, which prevented the *coup-de-grace.*
Alas, the real case seems to be different, and in its difference one feels that Lorenz may be breathing a sigh of relief, for he never seemed comfortable with his conclusions, and privately wondered why *Homo sapiens* should be so different from his animal brethren in this respect.

Many subsequent studies by ethologists, primarily in the field of ape behavior, have shown that the human is not the only animal that kills his conspecifics with malice aforethought and with glee. Jane Goodall's observations in Africa, now spanning two decades of life among chimpanzees, verifies that these, probably our closest animal kin, will sometimes purposively kill each other's offspring and do so from motives of jealousy (analogy or homology?).[26] Other studies verify that, in this and other species, the first act of a newly installed dominant male may be the systematic destruction of his rival's offspring. Even the dove, the symbol of peace, will brutally peck another to death under certain circumstances.

Though some of Lorenz's conclusions and remedies to forestall a human Armageddon may now appear naive, the study of human nature owes as much to him as to any other scholar in this century. His work with animal behavior, specifically in the area of aggression as a species-preserving activity, has by extension opened portals of vision into our behavioral origins that no envious environmentalist can ever close. The momentum that he initiated, which has been reenforced by so much subsequent evidence, is clear: Intraspecific aggression in substantial portions of the animal world is, to a greater or lesser degree, innate; it serves basically a species-preserving function in that it provides for better breeding possibilities; far from being a vice, it is a necessity for species' continuation, and hence a "virtue"; and, finally, animals do control it, by various means, usually but by no means always, short of conspecific death.

If we human beings are part of an evolutionary, phylogenetic continuum, if we therefore share much in substance and form with especially the primates, is it absurd to suppose that in the matter of intraspecific aggression we are also akin to them? I will leave this question open temporarily.

In our search for the beast a final clue should be mentioned—the genetic connection. So much scientific data and analysis has been forthcoming in recent years from the burgeoning field of genetics that even the specialists are hard pressed to keep track of it. From genomes to phenotypes the terminology is confounding and the implications fantastic. This does not mean, however, that all but the specialist need be removed from considering and appreciating how this science is altering our view of ourselves.

Central to a contemporary theory of human nature must be genetics. Tumbling forth from the cracking of the DNA code has come knowledge and technology that now enables us to cut, splice, and recombine genetic materials, to artificially produce everything from human insulin to oil-eating organisms. The horizon of this technology is virtually limitless, especially when any laboratory can now, for roughly $30,000, possess a "gene machine" that can synthesize a fully workable gene segment in a day or less. But before the possibilities of future gene technology overawe us, we should pause and note the way in which genetics has confirmed our link with our evolutionary past. More than any other features that link can be summed up in one word—heritability. The capacity of an organism to transmit to its offspring, *ad infinitum* part of its own form and substance, by means of an ordered, determined array of chemicals is mysterious enough; but that discrete organisms should share these enzymes and molecules, albeit in differing patterns, indicates what our primitive ancestors seemed to know intuitively—that all life is somehow one, different yet the same. Adaptation to environment, or as some would say, life-form, contributes greatly to mutation and change, both rapidly and slowly. But the cell remains, with its nucleus, and in that microcosm persists the record of our past and in so many ways, the history of our future.

IV

Ecce, Homo Politicus

Self-love and social at
her birth began.
Union the bond of all things,
and of man.

Alexander Pope
An Essay on Man

Human beings are born into, nurtured through, and laid to final rest in the company of their own species. Like countless other species, their existence is largely defined, for themselves and in the view of their conspecifics, by the group or groups to which they belong or from which they are alienated or estranged. *Homo sapiens* may be described partially at least as a participatory or belonging being.

More so than any other species, the sheer magnitude and intricacy of our participation with others of our kind distinguishes us as unique. The size of human groupings is varied, emanating out from family to "kin-clan," to identified community, to a perceived oneness with all the members of our species. The structural forms of human groupings not only vary from small to large to enormous, but are marked by different degrees of loyalty to the various forms of which we see ourselves a part. Hence, while we perceive ourselves to be members of the "human race," we tend to identify ourselves and our interests more closely with our country, still more proximately with our town, and most intimately with our immediate family or kin.

This capacity to identify as conspecifics in ever-increasing sized groups, along with an inverse bonding of mutual interest as the human group size increases, is a readily observable phenomenon or condition: The larger the group of which we are a part, the less identification of mutual interest and hence "loyalty" we feel. If we wish to make this a rule or maxim, we could state it thus: "The greater the quantity of group size, the lesser the quality of individual affinity to the group." This is hardly a major revelation but it is well to keep in mind as the following discussion unfolds.

Recognizing the scope and depth of human affiliation, Aristotle attempted to make sense out of a truly "one" versus "many" opposition. He decided to describe the human being simply as a political animal, later adding to this, a political animal that communicates complexly, that is, with language. He made this decision because his observations revealed that humans "normally" resided in the company of each other. So consistent was this pattern that he termed those who lived outside of a human community *idios*, not typically human, either lower beasts or, at the other end of the spectrum, gods.[27]

The distinctively human community he termed the *polis*. The usual translation of this word as city-state radically fails to convey its full meaning, for these words describe a formal locale but portray little of what Aristotle intended beyond that. Certainly he was referring to a physical location, a definable area in which people cohabitated. But the breadth and depth of human intercourse involved far more than mere physical proximity or institutional formality. The *polis*, the truly and distinctively *human* community, was an organic structure of human institutions, passions, contrivances, hopes, realizations—and language. To be human for Aristotle meant to do distinctively human things, and the demarcation between humans and other animals was the ability to convey ideas and judgments in a complex, nuance-laden manner. Where was this human ability exercised and manifested?—only in common interaction, in a communality. Hence his disdain for the hermit or shepherd, who, with human potential, nonetheless chose or was forced to live without human company. Such a person was no better than the beasts whom he tended.

A distinguishing characteristic of Mediterranean life, from classical times to today, is the preference of that

area's people for communal living. From the Iberian penin-
sula to the Near East the picture is the same, in city, town,
or village: a central square (or squares), the locus of everything public, from town hall, to markets, to cafes, the
human lifestyle is evident—constant talk. And the village
is the central human feature of the surrounding country-
side, stippled as it is with farms—but rarely with farmhouses,
for the farmers who work their land do not live in isolation
on it, or if they do, they are close enough to town to
guarantee a daily visit to it. The day's labor can be forgotten
and the spirit refreshed by gossip with friends over a few
glasses of wine. And so it was over two thousand years ago,
when Aristotle explored his more than 150 Greek *poleis*—a
usually walled or fortified town with its *agora* or marketplace, a focus of human activity and discourse.

For Aristotle the phenomenon of human communication
was so singular as to itself set the species apart from other
animals. Human beings could be adequately described as
animals who engaged in the distinct but related activities
of conceptualization and communication of complex symbols, with others who were capable of doing the same,
within a *polis.* Hence his definition of the being as a *polis*-
residing creature. The *polis* was at once that amphitheatre
within which singularly human activity took place and at
the same time the very reason for the activity. Hence, this
animal pictured without (that is, *outside* of and not in
possession of) the *polis* was not fully human because it was
absent from the vehicle through which its humanness
could be expressed. As such it would lack all rationale for
the exercise of that capacity which marked it in the first
place as distinct from other species.

Viewed in this way, the *polis* is truly the human womb
that replaces and transcends the biological womb of human
gestation. There can be no question of its necessity or
"naturalness" for the species: It is not an accidental contrivance nor a purposely willed construct; it is an essential
element of being human.

What I believe Aristotle was seeking to express was a
concept that would explain why humans lived together,
voluntarily and usually in peace with one another, coopera-

tively sharing, while at the same time seemingly pursuing their own happiness as they individually defined it. So remarkable was this characteristic of the human being for him that he could not conceive of full humanity without it. The *polis* was the organic reality of human speciality— neither beasts nor gods needed to apply.

Whitehead once observed that the Greeks may not have had all the correct answers but they did at least ask all the right questions. In the case of Aristotle, this is certainly the case, for implicit in his questioning, and in his definition of human nature, was a demand that the creature can only be understood as a totality, and that such a complete knowledge will only be forthcoming after a primary knowledge of its biological components were obtained. He did not presume that the human mystery would then be revealed in its fullness, but he did correctly imply that such fundamental knowledge was the *sine qua non* of any attempted final definition. Aristotle offered an implicit challenge to those of us who would seek to define human nature in its variable uniqueness: Seek that distinctiveness from a basis of sameness with other living beings and, once that is established, human nature will emerge from the contrast. He also implied that only empirically verifiable evidence was acceptable in this particular courtroom.

The rationalist tradition, of which modern political and social philosophy is in many instances the unhappy heir, insists that our life together is explicable in formal, structural terms, a contract among participants which is verified and signified by the "state." This abstraction of the "form" from the substance of our existence in common minimizes to the point of trivia the bonding element that both causes and explains why we live with (and occasionally fight with) members of our own species. Hence, few if any modern theories of the state can adequately explain our communal behavior because they ignore the obvious fact which Aristotle perceived—states, that is, "regimes" or forms of authoritative relationships, may come and go, but the *polis* remains, and it does so because it is itself the glue which binds us together. The *polis* is certainly a structure in that it has a structural form, for example, identifiable boundaries. But in addition (and perhaps, foremost) it represents the preconscious limits on human activity, adherence to which guarantees human and humane existence, success as a species—and rejection of which constitutes failure. When expressed, these limits become the norms or values that shape and channel human activity; in further refinement and final articulation, the norms become the laws of the polity. To add a gloss then to Aristotle's description of us, I would say that we are a "normative" animal, and that to be political means to be normative.

That human beings conduct their lives in reference to standards, norms, or values, thereby setting limits on their own and others' behavior, may seem obvious, as well as is the fact that the institutions of public order, including laws, are the reflections and specifications of this public morality. What is not acknowledged, however, is the innateness of these norms, their consequent universal pervasiveness, and their internal consistency within human groups.

The term "public morality" is rather out of fashion today, having a vaguely conservative, if not faintly medieval, taint or connotation. With some deference to lingual fashion, I insist that this is an appropriate term to describe the general (albeit often unquantifiable) body of values to which a community adheres.

If the term is invoked today, it is done so to describe a sensed public attitude, varying in meaning or understanding from opinion of the moment at one extreme to a *Weltanschauung* at the other. The former implies transience, flexibility, even frivolity, while the latter specters dogmatism, rigidity, and threatened irrationality. Between these extremes are variations of definition that include "consensus," "national consciousness," "community principles," and others. What these various understandings share in common is an unexpressed but nonetheless real assumption that "the" or "a" public morality is a construct of conscious human ingenuity, a kind of value-blueprint which has been designed, refined, altered as whim or reasoned need has dictated. How else to explain the apparently near infinite variety of human values, guiding principles, and moral injunctions which societies have and do offer as rationales for their institutions and actions? Does not the myriad moral expression among human beings testify to the oft-observed human capacity to adapt to virtually every change of environment and circumstance? The vaunted plasticity of the human organism seems eminently reflected in our different cultures and the public moralities which support them. Variation of moral (normative) systems is to be expected from a creature so malleable as to inhabit successfully every niche of the planet and so clever that it can now create new forms of being.

Coincident with and supportive of this view of human normative systems as variant and relative is David Hume's critique of Rationalist epistemology and the evidence accumulated in recent decades by cultural anthropologists. Hume's critique appeared to lay to rest the *a priori* presumptions of Rationalist moral absolutism and in doing so demonstrated that an empirical theory of knowledge must perforce acknowledge an insuperable gulf between fact and value. The logical conclusion was skepticism of the existence of an absolute objective moral order or at least our ability to perceive such, if indeed it did exist.

Theoretically, the position of moral neutrality for empirical (natural) science had been established. With the pretensions of cultural anthropology to the status of science, generations of modern investigators of primitive cultures have apparently confirmed that cultural and moral relativity are indeed fact—Hume's custom and convention as the sources of human value systems seem confirmed. Overarching these twin pillars has emerged the theory of natural selection in its original Darwinian form. The parts have produced a whole that then serves to verify the individual parts. Evolution means adaptation and variance, in effect, apparent organic relativity; skepticism logically permits only moral neutrality; and anthropological evidence "proves" the relativity of moral systems. This is, indeed, a formidable and complex edifice of mutual support, compelling among other conclusions that what constitute the operative norms of *Homo sapiens'* cultures are of its own conscious making.

At first glance, it may appear that Aristotle, if not a

kindred spirit to this line of reasoning, would at least be sympathetic to some aspects of it. After all, a relativity of norms or public moralities could well be fitted to his notion of various constitutions, and their resulting "regimes" or governmental forms, as the consequence of human adaptation. For Aristotle, the term "constitution" is really more equivalent to what I call "public moralities"—the warp and weft of values and conventions within a human group. Hence, his study of various constitutions was similar to an exercise in comparative cultural anthropology with the focus on differing power-authority relationships.

There is a crucial difference, however, between the approaches and conclusions of Aristotle and those of modern cultural anthropologists. Whereas the latter, at least until recently, have been content to record the differences among human cultures, stopping with the obvious variation, and concluding to a universal relativity, Aristotle sought to distill from observed variation some underlying, general or universal similarities. Thus, in spite of enormous accidental differences among human societies, he discerned fundamental or essential characteristics, general well-springs of human reason and emotion. This is not to say that modern social theorists, from Machiavelli through Freud have not also postulated underlying general principles of behavior and motivation, but they have done so largely without scientific rigor and hard data on the one hand, or as simplistic afterthoughts on the other. Even Aristotle himself, in a lifetime of attempting to distinguish the substantial from the accidental, succumbed to chauvinism in pronouncing that all non-Greeks were barbarians. Nevertheless, his effort and direction, if not always his heart, were in the right place. With all that they were and might strive to become, human beings were first of all political animals, that is *polis*-residing, norm-directed creatures. Their *poleis* and norms might differ superficially, but essentially they were the same. Hence, if Aristotle were alive today, equipped with the new biological data, he would agree with the observation that a political system, though ultimately much more, is first of all, a breeding system.

I have already noted that classical human nature theory,

in many instances best expressed by Aristotle, is quite inadequate in light of our contemporary knowledge of living organisms. But in the matter of succinctly describing one of the more singular ingredients of human life, he remains unsurpassed. Marx and Freud, both of whom were properly immune to the atomized individualism of Hobbes, Locke, and their Rationalist successors, who shared with our earlier tradition an appreciation of the human as a social, communal creature, nevertheless could not bring themselves to define *Homo sapiens* as distinctively a political being. Indeed, for Marx, politics and its baneful products, among them law and police force, were tangible evidence of our species' loss of natural innocence. For him, a political being was merely a synonym for an alienated, disenfranchised, class-ridden being—the victim of a system of exploitation.

The reason for the modern rejection of the term "political" as a synonym for "human" is largely due to historical circumstance, and with it, a change and loss of meaning. It is impossible to pinpoint when exactly this occurred but it must be largely attributed to the centuries' long disintegration of the Roman Empire, the fragmentation and rearrangement of loyalties in that aftermath, and the search for new definitions to describe the limits of power and authority. In no small measure it was also due to the absence of Aristotle's works for over a thousand years in Western European intellectual life.

In a European society, largely bereft of any central authority, in which the masses' obedience was continually vied for by clergy, bishops, and popes on the one hand, and nobles, kings, and emperors on the other, where anarchy was more in fashion than order, it is small wonder that the richness of the phrase *Homo politicus* was lost—as was the bulk of Aristotle's writings. Why Plato's survived and prospered in another form through Augustine, while his great student's did neither, except in the rich Arab culture of the Near East and North Africa, remains an historical puzzle. We do know that by the twelfth century European scholars could once again ponder his ideas, and that Thomas Aquinas so highly revered his work that he referred to him in his own writings simply as "the Philosopher." We also know that when Aquinas came to repeat Aristotle's definition he used the term "a *social* and political animal." It is a significant addition, this word "social," for it clearly implies that "political" alone could no longer fully express what Aquinas knew Aristotle to intend by that single word.[28] "Political" had already attained a modern meaning, more formal and less substantive than in the Greek of Aristotle. In subsequent centuries the term was narrowed further as the nation-state became the formal expression of public power and loyalty. From Marx's perspective, politics *had* become an alien and artificial concept and political animal an empty description.[29]

But Marx was not alone in his disdain of politics, now viewed since Machiavelli as the manipulation of power for private or public gain. While Hobbes bled the notion's substance by reducing it to an instrumental force to control basically aggressive and self-aggrandizing instincts, Locke formalized it further by advocating a "do-as-little-as-possible," night-watchman state. The American Founding Fathers, heirs of Lockean liberalism, were in the main as fearful of unrestrained popular power as they were of unfettered government. With the success of laissez-faire economic theory and practice in the nineteenth century, the final isolation of politics was achieved. The term no longer connoted the various aspects of a full public life nor even a view of the human being as a public creature. As morality, linked with religion, now came to be regarded as a matter of private commitment, so too, commerce became an issue of personal concern. War could unite citizens for a common goal but the unity was viewed as *ad hoc*, temporary, and like government itself, a necessary evil. The ideal became individual goals accomplished through personal courage and skill. Though now reviled as an anti-liberal image, it was really the superman of Nietzsche with his Promethean struggle against the odds and the gods who epitomized the liberal hero of the nineteenth century. The much-vaunted individualism, spawned of the Renaissance and Reformation, had fully matured. In this respect, Marx's view of a pre-political, though generously social human nature, was far closer to the classical vision than his non-socialist contemporaries.

When viewing the transformation of what it meant to be political from fourth century B.C. Athens to the contemporary global society, it is important to note that a glimmer of the former has remained in the spectrum of the latter. German Idealist philosophy, in so many respects a product of its own authoritarian environment, kept alive the perspective of the person as a citizen of the whole. Against the rampage of French Revolutionary individualism and the ironic skepticism of Hume, G. W. F. Hegel pronounced a pox on both houses with his elaborate metaphysical theogony.[30] In this battle there were no winners or losers since the contestants who were facing each other were centuries apart in time and on different intellectual battlefields—not surprisingly, they did not meet head on.

What Hegel restored to European philosophy had been anticipated, however, by Rousseau a century before, namely a sense that the person cannot be viewed as an individual, naked of its history as a social (and political) being. In one of Hegel's many dialectics he describes the person, automatically from birth a part of a family, surrounded by other families, all organized by some form of political order. The whys and wherefores of Hegel's reasoning and conclusions are not as important here as is his reassertion of the interdependency of humans upon each other—in effect, their individual incomprehensibility if viewed without others. The echo of the *polis* is clear.

Jean-Jacques Rousseau, that erratic doyen of so many creeds, which, if given a choice, he would probably never have espoused, wrote grandly in the eighteenth century on behalf of both sides of the fray.[31] On the one hand he lamented the demise of citizens' "natural" freedom and their enslavement by the institutions of their own creation, while on the other he warned against a tyranny of the majority in public decisions and invoked a "General Will," a public morality, as the final embodiment of a "common good." Though without question an advocate of individual freedom, Rousseau refused to abstract the person, as citizen, from the natural, social compact.

Even more so, Hume, a century later, scoffed at the idea that humans ever did or could live in anything but a communality, the values and institutions of which were the result of generations of trial and error. For Hume, customs and conventions were the roots of human behavior, a view eloquently espoused by his contemporary Edmund Burke,[32] though for much different reasons.

The disembodied, rational eyeball of Rationalism, the abstracted person of lone pursuit, was not, therefore, the only prevailing view of human nature until the twentieth century. Indeed, an intellectual lineage can be traced from Rousseau, through Burke and Hegel to Marx, with Hume standing, probably smiling, on the sidelines.

The irony in this contest to describe both human nature and politics is that, in their efforts, neither side seemed willing or able to strike a balance. The individualists, with the solo person as their premise and freedom as their goal, could not tolerate even the whisper of governmental intervention; the communalists, viewing the person as part of an organic, social whole, logically stressed obligation and responsibility to that body, most often at the expense of personal integrity. Rousseau, with typical ambiguity, could speak for both views when he declared that if he were in error in his understanding of the common good, the individual would be "forced to be free." With such a background, it is hardly surprising that the contemporary successors of both persuasions can find little common ground for agreement when one side calls liberty "freedom from restraint," and the other sees it forthcoming only through subsumption in some mythical whole. Little wonder also that politics is no longer seen as a necessary natural essence of human existence, but rather is consigned to a narrow, functional means of gaining and using power. The classical "Golden Mean" of harmony and balance in human nature has gone the way of the dinosaur.

These observations are not a lament so much for the passing of a particular view, the *Homo politicus* of Aristotle, as they are for the absence of a definition in modern political philosophy that accurately describes the creature. The *polis* in its original form may be gone, but is the creature of the *polis* no more? Today we have nation-states and in a recent yesterday, kingdoms and empires. Our environment is far different as is our capability to use it and shape it. The characteristics of our "regimes" or governments are vaster and more complex, our capacity for communication more extensive, as is that which we actually communicate. And, of course, our means of aggression against each other has increased geometrically.

This distance from the Greek political person has led us to view ourselves as at one pole or another: the singular hero of the liberal vision or the passive Eloi of the conservative fold. One view exhorts us to change our lot if we are unhappy with it; the other warns us to, like the shoemaker, stick to our last. And both disagree as to when and under what circumstances we should do either.

Trapped between these two extremes of modern ideology, neither of which has provided a convincing epistemology, I must question if perhaps both are inadequate in their understanding and statement of what I and my conspecifics may be—and can strive to be. May one's ardor for the enhancement of freedom have caused a myopia that blurs the necessity of cooperative human intercourse over time, while the other's overconcern for stability loses sight of the thinking, striving individual?

The modern views of human nature and of politics have fatally erred in their overemphasis of one observable aspect of human nature to the exclusion of the other. The *polis* of the Greeks is gone in its superficial form but its substance, the human being, its simultaneous creator and creation, remains. When Aristotle described the person as a *polis* being, he was defining not just a Greek in a Greek community but a human in a human community. The passions and drives of individuals, their reason and instincts, were combined in a locus shared by all of the species who wept and exulted, who conceived and nurtured offspring, who shared and connived, lived and died as humans together. Regardless of the form of the *polis*, its substance remained the same. And, indifferent to all subsequent efforts to divide us from each other, or to combine us anonymously, we have remained as Aristotle saw us—we are "ambiverts."

I have chosen this term as a description of ourselves in our behavioral modes for it signifies us in our fullness while recognizing our two major parts. The ambivert is an organism that strives to maximize its own individual needs and desires as it perceives these, while at the same time, carrying on this pursuit in the company of others like itself, all doing the same as it. Biologically, the ambivert is one, a single, a unique—the gentic mold was broken when sperm invaded ovum to produce a zygote—unlike any other before or after; but that very creation of the one required the action of two of its own species, each of a different sex. From conception, the one is not only caused by others, but dependent upon others for its very existence, and ultimately the fulfillment of its individual satisfaction. For the one, others are, through its existence, its boon and its bane, for it must exist and prosper through them, and often, in spite of them. From this all too human condition—an inescapable and fundamental fact—springs potential conflict, as well as individual satisfaction, and with the presence of both, politics.

The ambivert is torn in two different directions. It strives to survive at the maximum comfort level, but in its quest continually encounters others doing exactly the same thing. Yet, ironically, its world is not simply an opposition or competition against or between itself and others, for in most respects it needs them, as they need it, in order to fulfill themselves. Sex is better, food more varied, shelter safer, experiences richer when shared with another or several others. And the company of humans bears witness to that most human of all endeavors—language.

In our ambivertance, we are like most other animals which reproduce sexually. Among our nearest relatives on the phylogenetic ladder, the monkeys and apes, only the orangutan leads a largely solitary existence, though even it needs one of its own to reproduce. It is obvious that sexually reproductive animals must come together for mating purposes and that many remain together, at least through the nurturing and maturing periods of their offspring. But what requires them to remain social after the necessities of propagation have been met? The obvious answer is that sociability provides individual and group protection and satisfaction.[33] The advantages of togetherness far outweigh its disadvantages in the struggle to maintain existence and to perpetuate the individual's genes in future generations. The herd, the pack, the kin-clan, and the extended family are nothing if they are not first and foremost the vehicles through which the one extends and maximizes its life in and through concert with others. Societies, large and complex or small and simple, are easily seen as breeding systems in which all share and prosper to a greater or lesser extent. Their personal prosperity will depend upon their rank or status, vis-à-vis the others. Thus, the silver-back male gorilla, head of an extended family of females, young adults, and infants of both sexes, possesses exclusive sexual privileges with the females during their estrus. It is his reward for the role of protector and provider that he performs for the group—and guarantees perpetuation of his genes through his offspring. The pattern is the same among many other apes and monkeys, canines and felines, antelope, deer, and countless other mammals. Though the dominant male receives deference from his group, reflecting his strength and prestige, he rules like a truly benevolent despot and all benefit from his forcefulness: Females and offspring are protected from predators and inter-group strife, while younger males have a role model from whom they can learn until such time as they leave the group in search of their place in another family.

The peace and harmony, the succor and cooperation that enable one generation to create the next is purchased at a price. The cost is dominance through force, imposed by the stronger upon the weaker to maintain a hierarchy in which the interests of all are served by all, but in different ways and to different degrees. The catalyst of life within the group is competition, primarily competition to breed successfully, and that competition will inevitably result in conflict.[34]

One focus of conflict will be territory, the most advantageous locus for breeding and eventual nurturing. The marking and defense of a territory is a prerequisite among many species prior to the mating ritual and its consummation. In simple terms the strongest and most able males procure and defend the best territory, attract the most and/or best females, and successfully reproduce.

But among social animals in which the breeding structure and hierarchy is already established, conflict is also potential, that is, not restricted to the mating season. Here the phenomenon of ritual takes over, the combination of instinct and "learned" or emulated behavior to which we can only give the title "rules." At the risk of anthropomorphizing, we might call it the animal group's "public morality." What else can it be called? If morality is the sum total of the mores, customs, and conventions of a group, passed on, revised, or abandoned, why can we not say that the rites and rituals of order in a baboon pack, for example, constitute its public morality? Its source may be more automatic, spontaneous, instinctual than in us, but the result and function are the same. It is the "do's" and "don't's" of the group, transgression of which brings swift retaliation from the group's enforcer(s) of public order. Anarchy cannot be permitted. The group must, for its survival, meet threats from predators or other conspecific groups with a solid front, while, within the group, instability will threaten the ultimate safety of all.

It was Lorenz who first fully formulated the difference between aggression of the prey-predator variety, that is interspecific, as opposed to that exhibited within the species. The latter, intraspecific, is intended to gain and retain dominance and to quell "public" disorder resulting from a breach of the accepted do's and don't's. As discussed earlier, his theory has been vindicated to the extent that now intraspecific aggression is accepted for the species-preserving function which it serves.

In sum, intraspecific aggression (or "aggressivity") is natural in many animal species and to be often expected in species that are sexual, in which competition for mates (often including competition for territory) is inevitable. Aggression may also be manifested for non-sexual reasons among species' members, again with competition as its

root. Peace and order are usually maintained by adherence
to the accepted rites and rituals of the group. If these are
not violated, conflict ensues. Most often, but not always,
the competition cum conflict is not lethal—the rites of
submission by the weaker to the stronger usually prevent
death. Order is restored. Aggressivity has preserved the
group, and by logical and actual extension, the species.

It is obvious that I intend what I have described of animal society to be a partial mirror image of human society.
No great intellectual leap is required to identify with a
pack of baboons or a family of chimpanzees. Let us count
the ways of our similarity. We are both primates and hence
mammals; we are therefore sexual; we compete for sexual
(that is propagational) advantage; we live together with our
kind, usually cooperatively, but we conflict with each
other in subtle and not so subtle ways; we seek our own
advantage constantly, but usually we do so within the confines of rites and rituals that we call norms and laws; we
mate and nurture our infants, change sexual partners or
bond to our mates for life; we kill each other, and at the
same time mourn for the dead. In short, we exhibit the
same urges and behavior patterns as our nearest primate
relatives. Yet, as close as they may seem to us, we refrain
from asking a chimp to dine with us, and not primarily
because of our fear that it might use the salad fork to pick
its teeth. It and other species, no matter how they may
resemble us, are not of us and (probably) never will be.
Their society, their breeding system,[35] is not a political
system.

I indicated earlier that Aristotle would have agreed with
the statement that the political system is a breeding system,
but he would insist—as do I—that it is also more than this
biological base. The political system is fundamentally a
society and in this respect it is like other animal societies
in which individuals come together to create an ordered
whole that will initially benefit them as individuals, and by
extension their offspring, and, ultimately and inadvertently,
the species. But this human society is not just the product
of instinct, though its origin certainly was. What has devel-

oped in addition to a propagative structure is an overlay, an addition, an extra dimension, the source of which lies in language and the distinctively human organ which in turn accounts for it—the big brain. Without fear of exaggeration or *hubris*, we may describe the political system as a unique form of society in which our greater human capacity to remember and to conceptualize adds a reasoning ingredient, which even our closest animal cousins do not possess, and which affords us the further luxury of choice—that is, commitment within a realm of reasoned alternatives. To choose, on the basis of calculation of various means to obtain our ends, is a truly distinctive feature of our species, It does not replace instinct but supplements, elaborates, and enhances our natural drives. It is the difference between a political and its root, a social system.[36] Hence, a political system is, indeed, a breeding system, but a human breeding system with all that that must imply.

A good portion of this implication can be understood in terms of my earlier, tentative definition, which can now be expanded. If we can view ourselves as an ambivert, a Janus-like creature pulled in two directions—the one a search for individual gratification, the other a need to cooperate with others—then personal assertion will inevitably engender conflict. This conflict will manifest itself both within the family and kin realm as well as outside of it and will take a form ranging from simple one-upmanship to outright dangerous physical violence. What maintains equilibrium within this system, what accounts for the fact that *Homo sapiens* has not destroyed itself over the span of its evolutionary coming to be, is its control of its own and its conspecifics' inclination to use force to obtain desired ends. If we lack the automatic and elaborate rituals of submission, which many mammals have retained, sufficient to forestall death and restore a peaceful order, we do, at least, possess an awareness of consequences if conflict continues unabated and the mental wherewithal to bring conflict to a halt.

The distinguishing feature of a political system is, therefore, the presence of political activity, which must be viewed as the human effort directed at the control of aggression or violence. This is the gloss on my earlier definition of politics as the reasoned control or resolution of actual or potential conflict and must be seen as the base, the *sine qua non* of the human, that is reasoned breeding system. Without the security for life and life extension which this complex interaction provides, there cannot exist those other human enhancements which we airily call "quality of life." "Freedom" and "happiness" are mere abstractions to the creature whose very existence is constantly endangered.

From this vantage, politics involves far more than the formal institutions with which we usually associate it. They are, of course, necessary but constitute merely the tips of the iceberg in human affairs, the most obvious, formal expressions of what is continually transpiring at the more local, personal level. We are all, always, engaged in compromising with others, in reaching accommodations with our species' peers and forestalling, avoiding, or resolving conflict with them. We have purposively contrived elaborate institutions and conventions to make this task easier, but in our day-to-day existence, we accomplish the same result on a more personal level—a smile, a handshake, an accommodating word, a physical retreat. In fact, biochemically and physiologically "backing-off" costs us much less in physical and psychic stress than does confrontation. We desire the whole loaf of bread, but at the risk of losing it all, we settle with others for a slice or two. Because we are ambiverts, we are in a condition of constant, regular, potential or actual competition and/or conflict. That our population now exceeds five billion is enough in itself to indicate that, by this measure at least, we have been successful in controlling our intraspecies' aggressivity and conflict.

On balance, Aristotle was probalby correct when he termed us a political animal, in the sense—and if he did, indeed, mean—that we are creatures who seek to maintain our existence individually and collectively by the vehicles that we have available to us—our big brain and its most formidable expression, language.

If we can accept our phylogenetic link with other living beings, then we must also acknowledge that we carry within our cells both our past and our future. We must admit that we are creatures of an unremembered origin who labor with a baggage train of instincts in our being, but who have also demonstrated that our unique biological apparatuses allow us to transcend the confines of a totally instinct-driven existence. We are ambiverts, like many other species, but with a special capacity to recall and to forecast, to reflect and to change, to reason and to will.

This is nothing more than an observation that we continually resolve the innate competitiveness of our ambivert condition (and its possible consequence, conflict) on a day-to-day basis, through a complex process of instinct, habit, and conscious controls. We are, indeed, creatures who early on learn from our experience, who are imprinted by parents, siblings, and society at large with the appropriate do's and don't's that will ensure our continued existence, and we, in turn, pass this accumulated wisdom on to our own offspring. We are animals who have much to learn from our conspecifics in the struggle to survive—but we are also biologically equipped with precisely the vital organ to enable us to learn the necessary lessons. In a sense, this is a kind of evolutionary "chicken-egg" situation vis-à-vis time sequence and cause and effect—without our unique intelligence we could not master the peculiar techniques of our future survival, which is threatened by a technology that is the product of that very intelligence. None of these observations are concessions to the extreme environmental behaviorists who categorically deny the instinctual substratum of our nature. Fortunately, these are becoming fewer. Quite the contrary, it is an assertion of the primacy of instinct in and through many aspects our ambivert nature. We are what we are as individually competitive yet socially bonded creatures because of that which we carry in the nucleus of every body cell. We are, as it were, a creature (like so many others) with dual programming—the individual or selfish, and the social or cooperative. Where we part company with other creatures is in our capacity to define, articulate, and pass on, generation after generation, the more sophisticated contrivances necessary to control our more sophisticated abilities for self-aggrandizement and destruction. This parting of the ways with other animals is simply the learned accumulation of the body-politic, the association of ambiverts in a reasoned breeding system. We are creatures of habit and convention, the latter being the body of rules geared to our own and others' survival. And all of this takes place in the company of others, a *polis*. This human breeding system is the intellectual-cultural womb, which supplements the biological womb of our gestation, and its vital "humor," the binding and enduring vehicle, is its body of norms and values, the public morality.[37]

V

The Normative Animal

Two principles in human nature
    rein;
Self-love, to urge, and reason,
    to restrain;
Nor this a good, nor that a bad
    we call,
Each works its end, to move or
    govern all:
And to their proper operation still
Ascribe all Good, to their improper,
    Ill.

Alexander Pope
An Essay on Man

Thus far I have occasionally referred to instinct, and facilely implied a homology between the automatic or spontaneous reactions of other animals—to fear, flight, or fight, to reproduction and nurturing of offspring—and ourselves. I have also contended that *Homo sapiens (politicus)* shares with other animals a social instinct, with all that this further implies for purposes of cooperation and conflict. That human social existence is of a more complex or different order, that is, political, serves to enhance that fundamental ingredient of innate sociability. It is time for some clarification before I explore the ramifications of these facts.

One of the longest running and least edifying controversies among social philosophers is whether human behavior is the result of instinct or environment.[38] The former view holds that human beings have innate drives, which, when triggered, produce predictable action; the latter position contends that their behavior is solely the result of external or objective forces which impose themselves on the organism and shape the resulting reaction. The stereotypical opposition of these extremes has been rendered as "nature versus nurture."

Both theories, in their extreme "either/or" form, have enjoyed historical popularity, but certainly the latter, best represented by environmental behaviorism in psychology, sociology, political science, and cultural anthropology, has dominated social theory in America in this century. The dogma has been accepted that we possess no innate instincts, only neutral drives, unformed receptors that will react to the stimuli provided by the environment. This conclusion has produced what I call "active, moral relativity," and its practical expression, social engineering. In retrospect this result was predictable, given the intellectual roots of the Enlightenment. But ironically, when Locke proclaimed that man was born with a *tabula rasa*, that blank slate just waiting to be written upon, the foundation was established for both major contemporary ideologies—Liberalism and Marxism.

Though their most passionate adherents may deny any common link, to do so is absurd. Both ideologies rely upon the presumed near-infinite flexibility of the human creature, a malleability seemingly reflected by the equally near-infinite variety of human mores and institutions or cultures in general. The facts seem to support both coincident visions of human nature, that we are a non-willing recipient of what our status and environment, at a given time, provides. Their further agreement extends to the proposition that destruction of the old, onerous institutions and the reasoned construction of new, more suitable arrangements will either restore us to a pristine natural state of "goodness," ususally defined as conflict free and perfectly cooperative, while providing the means for a willed progress towards infinite material satisfaction. Social engineering, that is, redesigning the human environment and its institutions according to a blueprint of future perfection, has occupied theorists and practitioners on both sides of this fence through the twentieth century.[39] Both ideologies also see themselves as antidotes to the silly extremes of nineteenth-century Social Darwinism.

Environmental behaviorism, as a fundamental view of perfectly plastic humanity, has been pressed into service by both Marxism-Leninism and Liberalism. The former has used it to justify "temporary" coercion by a self-declared party elite so as to establish a milieu in which future freedom will be automatic, while the latter has also sanctioned coercion, albeit more subtly, in the form of "freedom" of the marketplace on the one hand or on the other, government intervention to institutionally remove social inequity. In both instances, the key word has been "progress," a verb raised to the status of a noun, a process now become a condition and endowed with some vague moral purpose. Both declaim the virtue of progress while disagreeing as to what it is and how to obtain it.

The obvious failure of both ideologies to properly program the environment to produce the ideal social arrangement is apparent to all who have the sense to look. Contemporary Marxism is a ludicrous parody of its founder's ideals, while Liberalism in its two guises stumbles along, sometimes imitating its competitor (forcing people to be free—à la Rousseau), but most often urging its constituency to simply change its ways and lead a more "virtuous" existence.[40]

Not surprisingly, ideologues of both ilks are confounded by the resistance they encounter from those whom they wish to save. It is a curiosity why, with the best of intentions, leaders of both persuasions have been unable to convince their followers to follow them. The "masses" are, indeed, a contrary lot, seemingly unwilling to blindly place themselves in the hands of their self-proclaimed redeemers. Instead, these great unwashed seem as determined as ever to continue in their vile schemes to undermine the social progress so carefully planned for them. They remain obstinate at forfeiting personal property to achieve a greater, undefined communal good and equally unconvinced by laissez-faire promises; they refuse to limit their family size in spite of dire warnings of world-wide overpopulation and the consequent failure of resources to support them; and they remain unconvinced that the meek and forebearing will inherit adequate territory, much less the earth. In short, they continue to compete, often violently, for old-fashioned satisfactions and rewards with seemingly little concern for the long-term effects prophesied by their leader-planners. It is a bafflement to those elites of both camps that their fellowmen can be so obtuse as to what is good for them—as with Alice in Wonderland, it is a curiosity.

In concert with this general ideological leadership, the more particular academic guardians of human freedom and willed choice have manned the barricades against the theories of instinctual determinism for so long that they have lost sight of the fact that their antagonist is long gone, a victim of his own ridiculous and exaggerated notions of blind, automatic, response. The truth is that for a long time, no one, except for a peculiar small fringe, has taken seriously notions of Spencerian Social Darwinism.

An apparent contradiction of this statement, the phenomenon of Nazism in this century, is actually a case in point. By all but its most fervent adherents it was easily seen for what it was—a specious and illogical amalgam of pseudo-scientific theories of racial supremacy, assertions of pent-up national frustration, and economic chaos—all bound together in a demagogic package. The memories and shared guilt of the Holocaust are still fresh after almost half a century. Both should remain so, as well as memories of other evils from that tragic period of recent history. But it is a mistake to see Nazism and all that it wrought as primarily the extension of a hackneyed racial theory.

But the spectre remains and seems to constantly require exorcism far beyond necessity. Hence, honest attempts to rectify the exaggerations of environmental behaviorism have met with a level of vilification which would make Torquemada's inquisition green with envy—only the thumb screws are missing. Perhaps Lorenz, E. O. Wilson, and others have oversimplified or exaggerated in their own right the role of instinct in human behavior, but to dismiss their scientific data and many of their logical implications as the product of subjective bias is a distortion worthy of only the most fanatical ideologue. It also hints at the insecurity of their opponents who correctly fear that their own one-dimensional view of human nature can no longer withstand critical scrutiny. Their fear is well founded, for their work, insofar as it relates to an empirically based and holistic view of our nature, is proving to be woefully inadequate.

An obvious truth is reasserting itself. We human beings are neither identical to an ant or beetle performing in a programmed way, all of our actions informed from conception and determined to do those things which will perpetuate our species. Nor are we a soft, wet-sponge "mind," encased in a peculiar body, which simply does what it is told from the environment in which it finds itself. The reality is that we are both of these creatures to some degree—and yet more. We are part of the phylogenetic continuum and therefore we are animals with all that implies. We eat, sleep, defecate, and procreate. Like other animals, we adapt to our given environment, and continue in such, our animal activities. But, unlike our even nearest animal cousins, we consciously reshape our situation, redesign the landscape, redo the dwelling—literally, create a new milieu. We are both formed by our environment and at the same time capable of informing it to our preference. The net result of all this input and output is a creature which comes to a particular condition or environment, equipped with certain basic, unlearned survival skills (breathing, suckling), with the capacity to learn more of that which is required in order to survive for the sufficient time to propagate more of its own. What this curious creature does in the meantime is inform that very environment in which it finds itself—clear the trees, plant the crops, raise the animals, build the shelters, and fend off predators—all of which guarantee its temporal existence.

If aggressivity and territoriality are instinctive among other animals, along with cooperation and nurturing of offspring, why should not these activities also be instinctive is us as the fundamentally necessary means of assuring self and group preservation, propagation, and thus, species continuance? Once admitted as instinctual it is an easy conclusion that these characteristics are not going to be eliminated permanently by even the most robust social engineering techniques. But such an admission in no way challenges the species' extraordinary ability to shape, channel, temper, and expand its environment in terms of its instincts. In this dimension, *Homo sapiens* is both an affected and affective creature—shaped by and shaper of its context. We are normative animals.

If my view of ourselves is correct, it means that we are a creature not unlike others who share our habitat. We are territorial, aggressive, sexual, cooperative, and competitive. We call ourselves these things because we observe our interactions and name them thus. Our ability to do so has already been noted and ascribed to our possession of the big brain, and the wonderful products of that organ—thought, memory, and language.

But there is another characteristic of ourselves that we often overlook though it is perhaps our most crucially distinctive feature: *We* both create and are created by the norms which guide and drive our existence.

To say this is to note the obvious. Truth, justice, goodness, and beauty are words in every human culture's vocabulary. Their precise meaning or definition might vary, but the effort remains the same—to evaluate or make a qualitative judgment about the perceived reality. Such a judgment will be, of course, subjective, that is, personal, but if it is shared by enough of one's kith and kin, it is considered to be an operative standard. Families, villages, and towns, whole nations proclaim their intentions and prohibitions in terms of standards, the concrete expression of which are their institutions, rites, rituals, and laws. And what is the source of all this order (for ordering is what it is)? I believe that the most viable hypothesis is that the origin of human normative order can be located within the organism, not as a "soul" or "mind" but rather in a very tangible, observable entity—the human cell, or more precisely, its DNA.

When I say that we ourselves create our norms or values —that is, our morality—I mean this quite literally, but in a far different sense than it might be understood normally. We are the authors of the rules we live by, but that authorship does not have its seat in our consciousness alone nor even primarily. We have become so conditioned to accept the Rationalist presumption that we are a totally reasoning being, that infinite progress is within our grasp, and that we can make of the world what we want, that we have lost sight of a simple truth—human beings have acted alone and in concert over eons to achieve a singular goal—survival. In pursuit of this end, they have used the same normative means, though these have had many different guises at different times. The evidence of this is quite clear if we make the effort to perceive it. And when this evidence is recognized it forces consideration of a very startling possibility —that the roots of all human values systems lie literally in the biology of the organism.

Franz Boas, Ruth Benedict, and the perennial *enfant terrible* of "revisionist" morality, Margaret Mead, helped to create modern cultural anthropology and its reigning method, direction, and conclusions.[41] According to the prevailing wisdom of this popular school of thought and field examination, human societies develop their respective value systems or moralities in response to their specific needs and environments. Thus, coming of age in Samoa will be very different than the same experience on Attu in the Aleutians or in the African Ituri rain forest or in the Bronx. Different customs, rites, rituals will develop in answer to different needs and desires. Different situations and problems will require different solutions and institutions. Combinations of rules, conventions, and even languages are evidences of the human's fantastic plasticity and variability. Though inclined to fight and propagate, compete and mitigate, humans will do these and many other thngs in combination because they choose to do so at a particular time, in a particular place. And the place—the soft South Seas, for example—may incline its human inhabitants to a gentler way of life than the harsher or more harried environments of a cold climate or an urban, industrial society.

This mix of rites and customs—of ways of doing things— we have come to accept under the rubric of different "cultures" and further (depending upon the viewer's arbitrary criteria) as "civilization." All vary, and have varied from each other, in nearly countless ways. The variation has occurred because of the composition of their integrating factors, the times and periods of their inauguration, development, decline, and demise, and because of the environmental or ecological space which they occupy. This observation translates into the conclusion that moral relativity, that is, a consistently and constantly changing (or at least changeable) code of behavior is evident in human groups or *poleis*. Where Mead found sexual repression and conflict in America, Samoa offered its opposite. Something was "wrong" about American society that it should spawn and tolerate these ills, while all the time other humans were living a more "natural" (normal?) life in the South Pacific, a truly Rousseauistic state of nature. Mead spent most of her public career proselytizing for reforms of what she thought to be wrong or aberrant in American mores and institutions, as opposed to the more natural and open society of Samoa.

The dominant cant among cultural anthropologists has been an attempt to reveal the true human nature via a study of arbitrarily designated "natural societies," and to juxtapose these against "modern" societies so as to expose the evils of the latter while implicitly or explicitly espousing a return to the former. The state-of-nature mentality persists and is as far from the truth now as it was in its inception and halcyon days.

Cultural anthropologists correctly seek to induce generalities about human nature from the specifics of discrete societies. They attempt to find some underlying human activities and principles of behavior in primitive cultures which are applicable to the species as a whole. And in many instances they have succeeded. Too often, however, they have begun their work with the spoken or unspoken bias of Rationalist, environmentalist presumptions—humans are solely the product of their environment; though shaped, even determined by the environment, they can alter both it and themselves almost infinitely; and that reshaping can and will be done by enlightened intellect and good will. It is not that these premises are necessarily false as that they are incomplete. As such, they provide only a partial notion of what we are and perpetuate a romantic vision of what we are capable or incapable of changing. When such a popular writer in this field as Ashley Montagu can declare categorically that we have no instincts one can only conclude that the laborers in this worthy vineyard are ill-served, for certainly many of them must disagree. The basis of disagreement should stem from the historical and now recent biological evidence, which any contemporary philosopher of human nature must confront. Such a confrontation clearly reveals the incompleteness of the environmentalist position—that as variant as human value systems are and have been, they are at root precisely that—variations on several constant and consistent themes.

No academic degree nor long field studies of primitive peoples is required to discern what characteristics must combine in order to mark a being as distinctively human. Among these distinguishing features is the fact that they live, regardless of their locale, in various sized groups and according to certain rules or norms. These dictates, which order their lives, are customary, that is, handed down from generation to generation. They may change as exigency dictates but they do so slowly. Most importantly, however, they are the tip of the normative iceberg, the pale reflection of the underlying principles upon which human life and behavior has grown and prospered. In final analysis, they are the secondary products of the primary values which have thus far assured the species' survival.

Even the most superficial examination of human groups, past or present, reveals an enormous discontinuity or variation in the apparent values and practices to which humans subscribe. What else could be expected from such an adaptable species? A question cries out from this observation, however. Is this variation of human value systems a fundamental or merely accidental, superficial difference. In other words (or from another perspective), can different groups within the same species evolve or adapt to a differing set of values, norms, or standards for its behavior than its species' mates, for reasons of different environment? The ready, common sense answer, is "of course, why not, and isn't that precisely what our observation reveals?"

In answer to this, and to some related questions yet to be raised, the taxonomists who have declared us to be a separate species are thus far correct. We are *Homo sapiens* (and, *H.s. politicus*). Furthermore, cultural or value differences are to be expected. But the continuity and the consistency of the principles which underlie those customary variations are the stuff of our biological being. Underneath all the apparent variation between the "Eastern" and "Western" mind, among the cultures of one nation or another, there lurks a constancy that cannot be ignored—the fact that all members of our species seek first and foremost to survive and to this end have subscribed to a handful of primary principles which antedate subsequent, secondary variations.

The types of our survival techniques are as varied as we are, but they inevitably involve rules and regulations, proscriptions and prescriptions, which we did not have a part in authoring and may have only a small hand in changing. This is so because we are ambiverts, born into a *polis*, destined to be a political creature, a part of the main of human existence while yearning to be free of it. This baggage of our human condition can no more be jettisoned than can that genetic combination, the biological survival mechanism, responsible in the first instance for our values.

If we view ourselves as organisms which are equipped wih the tools to achieve our continued existence—what do we find? A rather fragile beast, vulnerable to heat and cold, devoid of fang and claw, prone to skeletal and muscular difficulties because we are only recently bipedal. But we have survived and prospered as a species because these comparative disadvantages have been outweighed by the advantage of our big brain. Through memory, calculation, and verbalization—all manifestations of what we term "reason"—we have come to our present dominant status in nature. But this cranial mass in its present form is a relative parvenu, a late-comer in our developing humanity. What it has enabled us to do is to merely articulate those necessities of behavior to which we already adhered long before we assumed our present human status.

Observation reveals the universality of human value or normative systems, that is, that all human societies live according to rules.[42] That same observation indicates that the rules by which we order our existence vary greatly. And further observation must lead us to conclude that our various normative systems are actually derived from a very small number of universal norms, adhered to in the main by all members of the species and directed as means to achieve a primary goal—survival.

The validity of this statement requires nothing more than a comparative analysis of human value systems. Such a comparison reveals that the several fundamental principles from which all normative variations of human morality evolve are alike in all human communities and can be reduced to the single proposition: "Do that which will promote life, avoid that which will cause death." To save ourselves a culture by culture comparison, we can verify this observation by examining a long-standing and familiar moral code, the Decalogue of Judaeo-Christian tradition. Its fundamental identity with other moral codes will be obvious.

I bluntly contend that the Decalogue, the Ten Commandments, is an example of a moral regimen, not of how human believers can win salvation and eternal life, but rather of how human beings have thus far successfully guaranteed their earthly existence. It is, in fact, an articulated survival mechanism for this life. Stripped of rhetoric, interpolation, and in some instances, faulty translation, it states clearly and simply the "do's" and "don't's" which, when followed, have assured human cooperation, communal stability, and predictability of behavior—the basic ingredients for survival and propagation. Consider its injunctions.[43]

The first three commandments deal exclusively with our notion of and relationship to the idea of a supreme being. One obvious, observable, and verifiable institutional constant in human culture is the species' practice of religious rite and ritual, and its members' belief in a hereafter. From simple burial sites of neolithic times, through the pyramids of the Pharaohs to contemporary "memory gardens," humans have made the statement of their belief in life after death, of the existence of beings or forces which surpassed their own perceived puny ability to forever forestall the coming of that grim reaper, Death.

Feuerbach and Freud, among many others, have offered interesting arguments on the origins of religious belief.[44] The former saw humanity as the creator of divinity, not vice-versa. The creature, abject in material misery, created an unobtainable ideal which it called god, which it then worshipped from afar as subject to object and from which it was permanently alienated. For Freud, the notion of god was also a human illusion of an almighty, all-powerful being, belief in which comforts us in our realization of our own vulnerability.

These and other theories view the human predilection for religion as the result of pragmatic necessity. In its dawning awareness, the species recognized the existence of forces and phenomena which escaped its understanding and control, but which it also perceived as having a life or death effect upon it. The sun with its warmth, the moon and the tides, the refreshment of nature provided by rain, the security of fire—these and other evidences of nature were beyond human explanation, much less susceptible of human intervention. What else could this creature do in the face of such obviously crucial features in its existence but objectify them as beings or entities infinitely removed from itself yet minimally comprehensible in somewhat human terms. Anthropomorphism of these deities would naturally follow, and sun-god, rain-god, and others would require their worshipful due. Be the deity conceived of as one or several, the duty to appease or propitiate was obvious. Their survival, in their own minds, depended upon it.

This scenario of the origin of religious belief and practice makes eminent good sense. Awe, even fear, and reverence in the face of the unknown are typical human responses, and it is instructive that as our knowledge of natural forces has increased, along with our ability to control the environment and protect ourselves from nature's whimsy, so too, has our notion of the supernatural become less anthropomorphic, less personal, and more abstract.

But what of the yearning for an after-life for an existence beyond the visible and obviously temporal? It is a view, a passion, distinct from, yet connected to, the belief in deity and the supernatural, and may be understood in part from the species' sexuality.

Long ago our organic predecessors forsook parthenogenic reproduction. Unlike the amoeba, which reproduces *ad infinitum*, one cell simply dividing again and again, our species is sexual and requires the union, fusion, of two genetically incomplete cells. When they are joined, the new zygote or fertilized cell, the now pregnant product of two otherwise cellular throw-aways, can become a unique member of the species. Sexual reproduction, therefore, means individuality. But the price paid for this individuation is a reduction of the organism's existence to a specific time span—it has a beginning and an end.

Among sexually reproducing animals a profound recognition of "end things" must be a peculiar ability for us, the reasoning beings. Other animals sing or howl, moan or low a seeming funereal dirge for their own. It quickly passes as the corpse remains unburied, soon to be food of the life chain—and its kin life goes on.

But this is not so for us. We mourn our dead, even when they are not part of our relationship but just because they are part of our species. We build monuments, simple and small or grand and large, to remind ourselves of those of us who have lived and are now dead. We view their tombs, actually or in our mind's eye. Ultimately, we know and recognize death—and we abhor it.

Given our innate cleverness to dispatch means to ends, and our loathing to become only a rotted mass of flesh and fluid, is it surprising that we should yearn to transcend this vale, to picture our often less than pleasant sojourn on this planet as a temporary trip in time to be supplemented by an infinitely extended bliss? In fact, we create for ourselves an afterlife. When our ancestors became conscious of their mortality, we shall never know. One fact is more than likely however: When that awareness dawned, it was surely accompanied by fear of the unknown and regret that life must come to an end. It is further likely that at this piont, our ancestors set their wits and imaginations to the task of overcoming the finality of biological extinction. Thus was born the idea of an afterlife, a transcendence of mortality, a continuation of life if only in an altered form. And with this idea, we created religion, to offset and rationalize our innate fear of the unknown.

This hypothesis of the origin of mystic faith and its enshrinement in religious rite and ritual is too convincing to be ignored because it offers a natural explanation for that which has long been explained only in supernatural terms. What must be added to this picture to complete it is a recognition of the biochemical origins of the animal fear reaction. Other animals sense danger and react with flight or fight; only we, faced with the danger of death, can cerebrate that fear and assuage it as religion. The ubiquity of belief in superior beings and afterlives is hardly surprising in a species so singularly equipped with the mental power to escape that danger which only it can so clearly see.

Neuro-scientists describe certain animal reactions as the result of what they call "hard-wiring," that is the neural response mechanism which will spontaneously function if triggered by appropriate circumstances.[45] Such a hard-wired reaction is fear. As humans we are not instinctively, genetically programmed to religious belief. That is the aftermath of our inherited biochemical equipment. It is the means by which our ancestors rationalized, dealt with, and escaped from a recognized terminal fate. Planted in the species' dawn, belief in the supernatural was conventionalized for dozens of millennia, and still serves the same function as it did eons ago.

From the primal fear of death, religious response arose, but the content and form of that response has evolved with enormous variation. This, too, is to be expected from a creature who, in the course of millions of years, has encountered near as many differing environments. But with an increasing reliance on science in general, and a greater control over the environment in particular, notions of an anthropomorphic deity or deities have receded along with confidence in life beyond biologic death. At least this is true for some, while for many, one form or another of religious belief continues to provide comfort and escape.

It is not my intent to disparage belief in immortality nor to deny deistic faith. However, it is imperative to distinguish the provable from the unprovable, the more likely from the less likely, or as Thomas Aquinas put it, the realms of reason and faith. What I am proposing is a natural explanation for a universally verifiable fact—*Homo sapiens* has believed in the existence of an order of being greater than itself, and in a life after physical death. Human beings are linked in a phylogenetic continuum with all organic existence and as such experience fear. Our unique biological apparatus, the neo-cortex, enables us to both perceive and understand death, and to imagine the means to mitigate or escape its finality. Thus, in time, we elaborated religion as one of several survival devices, have pragmatically fashioned it in different forms, and continue to adhere to it in varying degrees as a palliative and an underpinning for other values which also serve a survival function. Viewed from this perspective, faith in the supernatural can be seen as a perfectly "rational" (that is, intellectually reasoned) human contrivance, to some degree promoting the end of self and group preservation. The truth of that faith, however, remains unverifiable.

Our existence as a species is very long compared with our knowledge of its history. Hence, it may be difficult to accept the notion that religion has functioned as a life-preserving vehicle (albeit a psychological one) when the past six thousand years of the species' existence have witnessed such intraspecific cruelty in its name. The apparent contradiction dissolves, however, if we recall that within this very short period of time, while the human population soared, available, habitable territory shrunk. Increased proximity of human groups did not increase amity among them, but rather the reverse. As greater competition for ever-increasingly scarce resources intensified, it is nor surprising that leaders and masses alike would rely on their religions to justify the most extreme actions against rival groups. Our "history" is replete with so-called inhuman cruelty towards our conspecifics. In fact our ancestors were doing quite human things—tenaciously defending or aggressively extending their procreative range, and most often justifying it in the name of their god or gods. Our seemingly innate discomfort with the ambiguous and problematic was (and is) overcome by the conviction that our action is demanded by our true gods. When religious beliefs, inherently dogmatic anyway, become absolutized, ordinarily unacceptable behavior can be sanctioned. But this is true of racial, class, or nationalistic as well as religious fanaticism, though historically the last type seems the most perfervid. Perhaps this is so because it is easier to die or kill for the expectation of a heavenly reward than for an abstract ideal about which even the most dedicated secular fanatic may sometime or other entertain doubts.

Many writers in the last and present centuries have echoed Nietzsche that "God is dead." Most of them have concluded to this because we deem ourselves a rational animal, religion is nonrational, and therefore it is irrational to continue to believe. What they are really saying is that in their estimation, god *ought* to be dead. What the obituarists of god and religion consistently overlook is the fact that in relation to religion human beings are only secondarily rational. Deity, as a human construct, has been born of instinctual fear; human reason has intruded itself in the equation only so far as an imagined reality can serve a reasoned purpose or purposes—as a means to allay a perceived danger and as a justification for subsidiary societal norms and actions. Hence, until it is massively apparent that these ends no longer require such belief, the species will no doubt cling to it as a conventional wisdom in spite of its unprovable status. If and when the species decides that science and evidence should replace myth and mystery—that is, to supplant god in the human brain—it will most likely be, as I have suggested earlier, with that very brain itself. Though perhaps inevitable, this perception and declaration is probably more far than near in our future.[46]

VI

The Self-Serving Species

Remember, man, the universal cause
Acts not by partial, but by gen'ral laws;
And makes what happiness we justly call
Subject not in the good of one, but all.

Alexander Pope
An Essay on Man

Belief in and worship of the supernatural as a means of coping with innate fear of the unknown is not so readily recognizable as a survival mechanism as are the other tenets of the Decalogue. In this Judeo-Christian expression of three tenets it is identical to that of other cultures in other places at other times in invoking belief, respect, and reverence for a being or beings, supposed superior to our own. Not even in its arguable monotheism is this tradition unique.[47] Nor is the remainder of its prescriptions and prohibitions any different from the fundamental precepts of other human moral codes.[48]

The fourth commandment directs persons to honor their fathers and mothers. This is simple and straightforward. But it is far more than an exhortation to pay parental tribute or acknowledge filial piety to one's immediate forbears. To fully appreciate this instruction it should be understood as advice to give respect and support to all of our older kin, and by extension, attention to all who have preceded us on our temporal journey through biological life. Such an extension of the commandment does not dilute but rather enriches it and makes comprehensible why we as a species generally revere and willingly provide for our elderly whether related to us or not.

But why should we concern ourselves with those a generation or two or three beyond our age? If we have survived to independence we are our own mover and shaker of the environment with our own problems of survival and propagation. We no longer require the nurture of mother's milk nor our father's oft-repeated litany of survival skills. We have become our own person and as such presumably need no other. In our condition of ambivertance—seeking our individual goals and desires to the maximum, yet always failing that and settling for less, because everyone else is doing and striving for the same—we recognize our inability to survive alone or even with only a consort and our progeny. We need others as they need us. It is our human condition. We enter life at the bottom of our species' life spectrum—"mewling and puking babes," as Shakespeare describes us. We mature, live, and die, but our lives from the initial moment to the final gasp are enriched by those who have gone before us. And, in deference to them, we pay our homage.

In a simple society, the hierarchy of generational deference is obvious, and its relationship to biological survival clear. The father, mother, grandparents, aunts and uncles—as survivors—possess a wisdom to be shared, a knowledge to be learned, and values to be passed on. They are, in fact, our cultural survival vehicles because they are our knowledge banks, our value repositories. It is the older one who instructs the younger how to shape the spear, how to track the game, how to ambush the enemy, how to gather and prepare the food, make ready for menses, conceive, bear, and care for the next generation. It is simply a case of stored knowledge—and that is reason enough to respect and listen to those who have avoided or survived the dangers of life threateners, and lived to enjoy the chorus of life's sound, light, touch, taste, and smell.

To fail to pay attention to or take care of his or her own in their dotage not only represents a posture of ingratitude but is an act of potential fundamental damage to the species. It constitutes a break in the continuity of human, that is, political life in which sharing and mutual aid are not just "nice things to do," but are the basic necessities of survival, for the individual and, by extension, for the group as a whole. The younger generation not only is paying back what it owes to those older ones who helped it to survive but is setting an example for the next generation in its turn to follow. Thus, the polity is reinforced by a continual vertical and horizontal repetition of aid and respect, initiated from the past and extended to the foreseeable future. In fact, this uninterrupted flow of bonding goes a long way toward guaranteeing that there will be a future for the species. No one in the distant beginnings of our species held a formal class in child nurturing, parenting, or care and concern for those past their prime. How then can we explain the ubiquity of these phenomena in every human culture, at all times? The obvious answer, which does not stretch the imagination, is that they are of the very nature of the being, and as such are instinctive. The fact that they manifest themselves differently, take different forms in different contexts at different times, in no way mitigates the existence of the underlying general principle: "Take care of and respect those older than you, as they have done, and as you wish it done to you." Are there and have there been exceptions to the rule? No doubt, but that is precisely what they are—exceptions to the rule, which if it were not a rule, our species would not have become as successful as it has proved to be.

The next commandment deals with a subject matter so patently obvious for its survival virtue that it is almost banal to consider it at any length. The prohibition, "Thou shalt not steal" clearly and simply states that one and all are forbidden to arbitrarily help themselves to goods which are not acknowledged to be theirs. In a sense, it may be argued that this provides an implicit recognition of private property or ownership, but the implications are broader. Certainly it can be read as "Don't take for private use, without permission, that which is designated the private property of someone else." But it also means, "Don't take from what is agreed upon as the *public* fund of possession." In a highly communalized society, in which the sphere of private ownership of anything is minimal but the public use is extensive (animals, crops, weapons), arbitrary allocation and use by the individual is considered stealing—taking what does not belong to one. Even in our own highly privatized societies of America and Europe, the notion of public property prevails. Hence, the selling of public lands to private corporations for their own exploitation and profit is roundly condemned as tantamount to theft from the society at large. The moral outrage that runs through the writings of Marx is precisely to this point. For him, and those relying on his criteria, the capitalist system provided the means by which the property of the vast majority, defined as the proletariat, was stolen from it. Whether one agrees with his specific analysis or not, the general accuracy of his insight was correct—what is defined as mine or thine or ours ought not to be taken from us without our acquiescence.

Human societies universally accept the general principle that theft, when defined and discerned, is an act deserving of punishment under the laws of the group. To allow it to go unpunished literally provides a license for stealing, something no human society can afford, again for the most obvious of reasons: It would create chaos, competition run wild, strife, and generally the kind of unstable situation in which safety and security have vanished, replaced by unpredictability and danger—not the conditions conducive to the success of a group or ultimately its species.

Each society decides for itself what constitutes private and public property, what act or actions shall be considered violations as theft, and what punishments shall be proper for those deemed as violators. But all societies which survive hold to the value that theft, however defined, shall not be tolerated. The last commandment, prohibiting the "coveting" of one's neighbor's goods, can be seen as a kind of gloss or reinforcement of the ban on stealing—not only don't do it, but don't even consider doing it!

Another commandment, closely related to these two, is the injunction not to bear false witness against one's neighbor. Taken literally, this requirement has a distinctively legalistic tone about it, implying trials and courtrooms.

This is hardly surprising given the juristic persuasion of the Israelites. Read again in a broader sense, however, it can be seen as a general prohibition against lying, spreading, or abetting the spread of falsehood and deceit—in other words, "Tell the truth in all of your dealings with your conspecifics." Once again, at the dawning of our species' bonding in the primitive origins of communal living, it is impossible to picture a condition of consistent and widespread deceit. Those prime requisites for survival and propagation—security and stability—were and remain difficult to obtain and retain. Without mutual trust and confidence not even the smallest and most primitive polity could have survived. It is difficult to imagine a community composed of Cretin liars or Baron Munchausens lasting out a day. In many instances, however, truth-telling may not always appear to be advantageous, just as not taking what one wants, whenever one wants to, may seem to be disadvantageous. But let us recall our ambivert nature. One part of us is the individual, seeking to maximize private goals and desires at every turn, as is everyone else whom one encounters. Our public selves, that part of us constantly dealing with others who are dealing with us and each other, must compromise or perish in our selfish pursuit. Hence, we do not, cannot, always or even very often gain all that we wish, and if we try to, we must acknowledge others' license to do the same. But such an acknowledgment on our or others' parts is self-destructive. What all of our norms of behavior limitation are, in the final analysis, is a body of self-protective mechanisms that, if adhered to generally, will guarantee us (and others) part of what we need and desire. We play politics.

Why is it to our long-term advantage to tell the truth, though in the short term it may leave us with less than if we had lied? Because the lie cannot remain forever consistent with the observable facts and eventually one's deceit will be discovered exactly for what it was intended—an attempt to gain unfair advantage in the competition to survive. For such an attempt, one could pay a fearful price. Lincoln's observation that you can fool all of the people some of the time, and some of the people all of the time, but not all of the people all of the time was precisely to the mark. Consistent falsehood can rarely go undetected forever since the lie by definition involves a false statement of fact. When the facts are available for others to judge, they will, in effect, speak for themselves. Even the most elaborate deceits, purposely foisted by leaders on their followers and believed by many of the latter, are usually revealed for what they are.

Here a distinction must be made between sincere misunderstanding of the probable truth and conscious distortion of it. So engrained in the human response system is the necessity to be truthful and to expect truth from others that our lives are led on a day-to-day basis with the expectation that our intercommunication with others involves an exchange of truth—that is, discernible facts, reported honestly, to the best ability of the communicator. The students may suspect that their professor's interpretation is in error, but they do not usually suspect the teacher of purposely deceiving them. We read a train schedule and assume it to be accurate and well-intended, even when the train arrives late due to unforseen factors. And we take with a grain of salt the nightly weather report, not because we distrust the intent of the reporters to tell the truth, but because both they and we know that they are working with only tentative knowledge. In fact, we live day by day on the assumption that what we see, read, and hear is communicated to us by others as truthfully as it is possible for them to do so. An ordered, stable, and secure existence would be impossible without such confidence.

It is precisely because of this assumption of honesty in others' dealings with us and our tendency to usually respond in kind that discovery of conscious deceit is so repulsive to us—the same kind of response engendered in us when we discover a theft.

Truth-telling is therefore a natural expectation. We account for the mistake in judgment, excuse the unintentioned error, are skeptical of the source if that source has been wrong before—but we are far less likely to forgive the intentioned lie, perpetrated for personal gain or advancement.

* * *

When we move to the commandment dealing with sexuality, we encounter again a rather straightforward prohibition that complexly operates at a number of levels in the way that it enjoins human behavior. It is perhaps the most interesting for what it says, implies, and does not say.

"Thou shalt not commit adultery" means "Do not engage in illicit sex," which is sexual activity of a particular kind, namely, sex with someone else's mate. This is very important, for what is being explicitly protected is what I call "procreative integrity," that is, the sexual honesty and loyalty which is necessary to guarantee the lineage of offspring. King David sinned, not for lusting after Bathsheba, but because his lust was directed at a then other man's wife. The rule is clear in this respect: A male-female bond with the intent of procreation ought not to be intruded upon from without. Chauvinistic as it may appear, it remains an undeniable truth: A male is only certain that his mate's offspring are his, if he is certain of her sexual fidelity to him. And why, in the great name of survival, is it necessary that a male be so assured? Because he will be ill-disposed, especially under conditions of hardship, to expend his energy and expose himself to danger in order to provide for offspring other than his own.

The interesting though not surprising point of this commandment is that it is worded as it is. It does not say, "Do not have sex outside of the marriage bond," nor "Have sex only within the marriage bond with the intent of procreation." In this respect it is clear—husband and wife, be faithful to each other, while you are of the age, condition, and intent to have progeny by each other.

At its core the commandment makes sense only when viewed in terms of procreative integrity and then it makes great sense. Through adherence to it, the male receives assurance that his labor as provider is not squandered on any but his own. But what does the female receive as reward for her fidelity? Her offspring are hers, no matter who the father is. Again, we need not look too far. She gains from her loyalty the trust of her male consort and with that comes protection and provender for her and her offspring.

She and they are vulnerable and her fertile span limited by comparison with the male. She needs precisely those things which he can provide and she knows that he will provide them if he trusts her.

The family, then, is the natural and primary polity and interweaves with the necessities of truth-telling and not stealing, for a violation of sexual fidelity in marriage involves both theft and deceit. The female in her turn demands fidelity from her mate since his extramarital sexual activity may diminish his role as husband and father. Not only may he be killed by an irate cuckold, but he may produce offspring by another female, thereby diluting his concern for her and hers. Hence, the bigamist is not usually well tolerated in monogamous societies—unless he can provide equally for his additional family or families. In Islam, where the Prophet allows multiple wives, the rules to be followed are very clear: A man may have no more than four wives at any one time, and all must be treated with equal respect and provision. Muhammed recognized that these conditions would be difficult to meet by any but a wealthy man, and so it would not (as has been the case) be the common condition. In fact polygamy is typically allowed only in those human societies in which underpopulation is the norm and where a priority is placed on having as many male children as possible, again for survival purposes.

The matter of male promiscuity raises some other interesting points, however, directly related here. Why should virtually every society, past and present, tolerate to some degree a form of female prostitution? Even in those societies where it has not been openly sanctioned it has continued to exist covertly, stubbornly resisting all attempts to eliminate it. Is it possible that prostitution has evolved as a formal or informal convention acting as a safeguard to the integrity of the family unit? Could it be that it has provided a kind of natural sexual safety valve, especially in predominantly monogamous societies? Available temporary sexual partners for the male would actually be advantageous to the entire group in several ways. Unbonded males would be diverted from seducing already claimed females; married males' promiscuity could be indulged without disruption of the family bond's material provision; and the bonded female could be relieved of unwanted sexual activity during times of pregnancy and offspring nurturing. Hence, the male is temporarily released from his bonds of fidelity to the relief of both parties, without fear that his sexual activity will result in new children to be supported. If a prostitute should conceive, she could hardly identify the father even if she cared to, while her customers would feel no continued obligation toward her. Our sensitivity to the material and psychological exploitation of women, and the danger and misery which they often bear as temporary sexual partners in our society, should not blind us to the fact that prostitution is indeed the world's oldest profession and that its presence and longevity have obviously proven to be *not* destructive of the family. Indeed, its very existence may stem from the need to redirect, temporarily, the sexual drive of the male, thus actually sustaining the family as the context for acknowledged offsprings' nurturing. It is absurd to contend that such an institution could be the result of male dominance, perpetuated since time immemorial, over unwilling victims. The odds do not favor such a conclusion when our species' record is one of institutions retained or discarded in direct proportion to their survival value. Prostitution will only disappear when it poses a threat to human society—a condition which it has obviously thus far not posed—or ceases to provide some value, which it apparently has continued to do.[49]

What this commandment relates to, therefore, is not human sexuality in general but rather to a specific instance of sexual activity—marriage. This must be viewed for precisely what it is—a public ritual in which the participants pledge at least temporary sexual exclusivity for the purpose of the easy identification of offspring, should they occur. In most societies sexual experimentation before public bonding has been the norm, being not only tolerated but encouraged. So too dissolution of the union when its procreative purpose has been served is a common practice. One minor but instructive example of how deep seated is this urge for public, formal recognition of the sexual bond when offspring are intended can be seen in the contemporary fad of "trial" marriages—offspring rarely result and if they do, the trial abruptly ends with traditional nuptials. It may be argued that many persons do not marry, and many who do, choose not to have offspring. The species' record, however, is clear—enough humans have done so over time so that we now count ourselves in the billions.

The principle contained in this commandment is far from a gloomy anti-sexual prohibition despite attempts by religious puritans to make it so. On the contrary, it can and should be seen as an exhortation to maintain and continue that already natural institution of the family with all that that entails, in a recognition and support of one's direct and indirect lineage. That human society has evolved from extended families through kin-clans to ethnic groups with specialized beliefs and language systems is testament enough to the degree of human adherence to this principle. The forms of procreative bonding may and do differ, sometimes radically, but the principle remains constant.

I realize that these observations may appear to disregard the fullness of the human male-female relationship—what we call "love." This is not so, for how could anyone dispute the existence of the vast array and profound depth of emotions that characterize human sexual bonding within and without marriage. What must be grasped, however, is that the complexities and sophistication of human intercourse in all areas of interaction is a matter of degree and not a difference in kind. The life-long bonding which we observe among so many animals in disparate species is not accidental or totally unrelated to ourselves. The eagle, goose, wolf, and African wild dog—to name only a few— mate for life, share the tasks of parenting, and evidence affection for and protection of each other. Though a fundamental purpose for these animals is procreation, it is hard to conceive of their behavior as devoid of the extra dimensions of solace, comfort, and pleasure beyond this primary need. And so too for us, albeit in more extended and intricate ways.

But if a necessary reason for our sexuality, as for other animals, is propagation of a new generation, it must also be remembered that we humans possess an enhanced sexuality far in excess of that enjoyed by any other animal. Our biological equipment, as I noted earlier, allows us to add the dimension of recreation to procreation as an aspect of our sexuality, a freedom for extended passion and pleasure that is unique to our species. What must be recognized is the inseparability of these sexual functions. One is not "primary" (procreation) and the other "secondary" (recreation) as some traditional "natural law" views of human sexuality would have it. Quite the contrary, the two dimensions are parts of an integrated whole and it is the entire package that partially accounts for the evolutionary success of the species.

The vulnerability of *Homo sapiens* in competition with other predators is often noted: a lengthy gestation period, an even longer nurturing span, a soft skin, the lack of fang or claw, a smallness of size, and a slowness of gait—all of these and others have placed us at great disadvantage in the survival struggle. But a unique form of sexuality, creative of a specially improved context of bonding, and with this, greater protection for the pregnable female and her offspring, coupled and integrated with an enlarging brain—all of these together could and did offset the species' deficiencies. In the truest sense, our distinctive sexuality is an integrated cause of our evolutionary success.

Predictably, then, as our intellects expanded to a greater awareness of the relationship of ourselves to our conspecifics, and to the rest of nature, we articulated norms of behavior that would promote our survival and procreation. One of these norms was procreative integrity—sexual fidelity to the mate responsible for our offspring. And with greater complexity of our cerebral cortex there evolved a more complex awareness of the speciality of our bond, an enhanced range of passion and response—in short, what we now call love.

I have saved for final consideration that commandment which at first reading seems to contradict the pattern which I have developed in the others, namely, that they all refer to general principles, applied or formulated differently in time and context. I refer to the prohibition, "Thou shalt not kill." In this form or translation the injunction appears to be an absolute prohibition against the taking of human life, and as extended by some, any life at all. Read in this literal sense there could be no exception or qualification, and certainly this has been the interpretation of Christian pacifism for many centuries, an echo of the pacifism preached and practiced by various groups and religions in the East. But as is so often the case, things are not always as they appear.

When I began my analysis of the Decalogue from a bio-political perspective, I was struck by the obvious inconsistency that this one commandment, perhaps the most important one since it dealt specifically and in no uncertain terms with human existence, should unequivocally deny the permissibility of ever taking life. It seemed radically different from the other normative principles. "Don't steal" begs to be further defined by answering the question, "What constitutes stealing? Tell me what 'it' is that I may not arbitrarily take to my own, and I will not do it." And so, with all the other commandments.

In fact, there really is no inconsistency. The commandment as it has come down to us has simply been mistranslated. When the injunction was rendered from the original Hebrew into its first translation, Greek, there were two Greek meanings available: "Do not kill," and "Do not murder." The former was chosen over the latter, and a fateful choice was made. From the Greek to the Latin to English, in our case, Christians have been exhorted not to kill—and from St. Augustine on, Christian writers have attempted to reconcile this injunction with the reality of everyday life. Augustine's theory of "just war," and its later elaborations, stemmed from an uncomfortable guilt, a nagging tic, to justify what appeared to be part of the human condition—killing—with the prohibition of the Mosaic Law and the apparent exhortations of Jesus to forbear, to forgive, even to sacrifice one's existence in the face of lethal threat. But if the prohibition is rendered as it could have, and I venture for logic's sake, should have been, as "Do not murder," then the inconsistency with the other survival norms disappears. "Do not murder" is fundamentally different from a blanket prohibition against killing because the former means "Do not commit *unjust* homicide." All human societies possess such a norm, and for the most obvious of reasons—individual and group survival. Unjust killing of another human being is to be avoided at all costs, and a violation of this rule is inevitably the most severely punished, often with the sacrifice of the murderer's life.

But what is murder, that is, unjust killing? Again, time and circumstance—the society's ethos or public morality—will make this definition. Different circumstances, needs, preferences will dictate what a society can tolerate from its members (more accurately, what society's members can tolerate from each other) in terms of homicide. Defense of the group's integrity—territory, lifestyle or values—is universally recognized as necessary, and if this requires the killing of outsiders, it is accepted without blush or qualm.[50] Even Augustine and subsequent Christian just-war theorists found no problem with a "defensive" war. Within the human group, however, extensive adjustment rather than an even pattern is found with regard to when a member or members may kill each other without onus. These various patterns will change as the mores of the group change, which, in turn, will depend upon the group's evaluation of danger. As societies determine their internal norms of justice, so too, they will judge the appropriateness of homicide. Once again, we encounter a universal human norm, in this case a prohibition of homicide outside of the prescribed limits, with the limits themselves determined by circumstantial, that is, particular, societal judgment.

It is ironic that, but for an ancient mistranslation, the entire tradition of Christian pacifism might not have occurred. Yet that tradition has served to sharpen our sensitivity to cruelty that can be avoided, the truly "senseless" killing of our conspecifics, the needless destruction of human life. But the necessity still remains: Under certain circumstances of perceived threat to the group, either from within (the "criminal") or from without (the "enemy"), life must be taken but only if the prescribed norms of the society allow it. In the New Testament there are recorded the words of Jesus, pronounced in his Sermon on the Mount—they are generally referred to as "counsels of perfection." They are ideals that are romantically attractive, but which bear little if any coincidence to reality. To continually turn the other cheek or to expect the meek to inherit the earth is to believe that in the short span of two thousand years the species can voluntarily jettison reactions that natural selection has, over eons, "wired" into it. Of course, by means of our neo-cortex, our reasoning organ, we can choose to mute, even temporarily overcome, the triggered responses of our older organs. But our god-like brain remains a tyro when compared with them. Competition, struggle, even violence have marked our species' evolutionary progress. This is not a value judgment, merely a statement of fact.

The Decalogue (and its mirror images in all other human societies) is an adequate guide for human behavior simply because it is a reflection of human nature. It recognizes implicitly the urges and needs of the ambivert and states the general principles that underlie human and humane existence. Understood in its broader interpretation, it can be seen as a synoptic statement of what our species has been doing as a means of evolving to its present state. The Ten Commandments, therefore, so dear to our very short span as humans, in our own singular historical tradition, serves as a reminder of what we have been doing as a species —individually and in groups—all along. It is a reinforcing statement made when we in the West had become more sophisticated in our techniques of communicating, more settled than our distant ancestors in providing for daily and seasonal requirements of food and shelter, and generally more comfortable with ourselves in our confrontation with our environment. It is, therefore, a recital of principles, shared and articulated by contemporary literate societies in the non-Western world, and intuited by all other human societies, past and present.[51]

One characteristic of these norms is readily apparent but deserves an additional stress—they are expressions of the negative. Don't steal, don't lie—to your neighbor or your mate—don't murder, and don't commit sacrilege of deity. These are the minimal prohibitions or limitations on human activity within a polity that must be observed if the polity is to survive. These are *sine qua non*s of human existence and as such tell us nothing about the quality or substance of life—the "good life" of the poets and philosophers. It is the adaptation, the specifications, the varied elaborations of these basic principles that are the next step in human value systems. These are the conventionalized rites and customs that make explicit and concrete the primary "don't's" of the species' life. These secondary expressions are the means by which varied societies identify their peculiar and quite relative understanding of their "good lives." And it is these secondary *mores* which have so fascinated students of culture and led them to the erroneous conclusion that there is no consistent and fundamental *urstuff* in human nature, or more specifically, in human value systems.

What we see, then, is that the primary biological direction of human behavioral evolution has been survival and procreation. This has expressed itself in a handful of general, universal principles relating to lineage, property, and truth. These principles, in their turn, have been and are expressed customarily or conventionally in the public moralities of human societies. I am arguing that human normative systems contain a basic root—survival of the individual as one of many (the ambivert)—which proceeds ineluctably to include the group, and hence, the species; that in this truly political (because it is actually or potentially confrontational) setting, the human group operates, conducts its business on a day-to-day basis, with this ultimate norm or preference or value as its uppermost priority; and that human value systems in their variety ultimately rest on this.

An enquiry into our species' history reveals that we seek to maintain our biological existence, that we seek to extend that existence, and that we recognize its inevitable end, that we mediate our disputes over property and that the safest and most economical use of our energies in perpetuating our genes is by truthful communication with each other. What is left? Variations on these sub-themes may and are made, but the roots remain. No human society which has survived has been without these norms.

Since this seems to be the case, the question may be asked, "Why should these norms constantly recur, from time immemorial, in all human societies, regardless of civilizational level?" The probability factor is too high to be accounted for by accident. Since it is obvious that these norms do serve a species-preserving function, the answer to the question can only be that the species has evolved to its present point *because* of the species' adherence to them. They must, therefore, be viewed as vital factors in our evolution, no less significant than bipedalism, language, and our large neocortex. And as with these characteristics, which we had nothing consciously to do with, so too, our values evolved in spontaneous reaction to our physical evolution. How could it have been otherwise? The alternative conclusion would have to be that human beings, at some specified time, consciously decided to adopt these norms as life-preserving means, and that they did so in all of their groups, at approximately the same time and with the same conscious result. And such a conclusion again demands the question "But if so, then who taught the teacher?" Once again we enter the realm of fantasy when we conjure such a picture.

Our species' technological development has been uneven, which simply records that some groups, for example, invented and used the wheel and others did not. But regardless of civilizational level, all human groups abide by these general norms. How did they come by them, just as all members of the species are bipedal, communicate complexly in languages that vary greatly but which all share a universal syntactic core, and possess brains, which mark them as different from any other animal? The primary principles of human behavior control must be as natural to our species as our physical characteristics. In short, what we call our human normative systems spring from that same selective biology that sees us as the evolved creature we are today. They are at one and the same time a cause and an effect of our human condition.

VII

The Biology of Injustice

So drives self-love, thro' just, and thro' unjust,
To one man's pow'r, ambition, lucre, lust.
The same self-love, in all, becomes the cause
Of what restrains him, government and laws.

*   *   *   *   *

Forced into virtue thus, by self-defence,
Ev'n kings learn'd justice and benevolence:
Self-love forsook the path it first pursu'd,
And found the private in the public good.

Alexander Pope
An Essay on Man

We shall never know precisely when our prehuman ancestors first intuited that some of their actions were appropriate while others were not. It is most probable that it occurred simultaneously with the phenomenon of bonding, for bonding included sharing and cooperation, and, with all, a sense of aptness or fairness. The seed of awareness thus planted would flourish as language developed, and mature as a full-blown concept with the evolution of our brain. The notion of justice must, therefore, be as old as true humanity itself. In reverse fashion, just as we cannot conceive of ourselves as human without an opposable thumb, bipedality, and language, so too, we cannot picture the member of a human community, no matter how rudimentary, as devoid of a sense of right and wrong. If one of our hallmarks as a species is our normative ability, our capacity to conjure "oughtness," then the supreme criterion of normative judgment is our notion of what is just.

Observation confirms that human societies, regardless of their superficial differences, engage in justification—the process of relating their behavior and institutions to acceptable normative criteria. The "right" and the "wrong," the "good" and the "bad" are evaluative judgments made in terms of the conventional norms of the *polis*, the ongoing and superficially flexible public morality which forms the skeletal structure of the human community. Though what the nature of justice is, or how it should be manifested, may vary widely, one phenomenon persists with utter constancy—human beings agree that there is something which they call "justice."

From Plato to the present no concept has been dissected and defined more often by Western philosophers than this one. And understandably so, for it is the source from which flows all related notions of rectitude, legitimacy, authority, equality, and obligation between and among persons. What it "is" provides meaning for that intuited moral gnawing, that human sense of oughtness.[52]

In spite of attempts to personify it, it has eluded tangible description for the simple reason that it is not a thing but rather a relationship, a situation, a state or condition of or among beings, not a thing itself. Yet it is perceived to exist, and to inhere in human beings and to be manifested by them. Small wonder that in our efforts to understand justice, we have resorted to an extraordinary plane of thought and discussion—the metaphysical.

Socrates was not being purposely evasive when he recommended to his audience that it seek to comprehend justice by analyzing the actions of a just person. Those who performed just deeds did so because they were just, in that they possessed and were possessed by justice. In short, such a person concretely exemplified the harmony or balance of soul, the quality of proportion so dear to Plato's notion of perfection. One might read Plato as advocating all things proper and appropriate, souls and societies at peace within themselves. The problem is that one may still retire from reading Plato asking the initial question, "Yes, but what *is* justice?" to which the replies have been as varied as similar queries about truth, beauty, and happiness.

Herein lies the rub. Our observation and experience tell

us that these qualities most dear to us are ephemeral, transient, subject to the mood of ourselves or others, inconstant, and relative. What is considered good today may be condemned as ill tomorrow. Yet, even though we are nature's most curious and inventive creatures, who thrive on change and grow easily bored, we nevertheless cling to the constant, revere the traditional, and yearn for predictable substance in our lives. We prefer the steady course of affairs and lament the passing of the familiar. Not surprisingly, we would like to know once and for all what justice is—and for that matter, truth, beauty, and happiness as well.

An evolutionary perspective of our nature requires an admission. It forces us to acknowledge that at the most primary level of consideration we have evolved to our present level of speciation by consciously and unconsciously pursuing that which conduces to our survival and biological continuation, that is, we seek continued existence and successful reproduction. When I say "we" I do not mean each and every one or group at all times. However, the record speaks for itself: There are now more than five billion of us because most of our ancestors engaged in this pursuit. During this odyssey, the members of our species have declared a multitude of relationships to embody justice, and an equal array of behaviors to constitute just actions. In retrospect, the pattern displayed is often bizarre and contradictory, sometimes foolish and even deadly. What emerges is a consistent preoccupation with "the just" in human affairs and interaction, but with variable definitions of how the "just" shall be understood. We do call and have called justice by many names and have given its names many faces. As uncomfortable as it may be for us, as contrary to our yearning for absolute standards, as seemingly destructive of a universal morality as it may appear, the fact must be faced that we ourselves are the author of what we call justice. Justice, therefore, in the minds of its beholders, is relative to the understanding and the bias of its practitioners and proclaimants. Hence, the observable fact of cultural relativism requires the admission of moral or value relativism as well. In the pursuit of our species' goals, we have chosen various paths and justified them all.

What alternative to moral relativism can be proposed?

The most obvious is that which has been offered at many times and in many guises since Plato—moral absolutism. This assertion would have it that there exists a metaphysical, unchangeable, transcendental order of justice of which human notions of rectitude are mere reflections or incomplete variations on an absolute theme. Whether viewed as in the Platonic world of Divine Ideas, the Christian belief in an Eternal law of God, or a Deistic reliance on universal, natural Reason, the vision and hope has been the same— there simply *must* be an absolute, final guide to human action, a natural law of human behavior which is as certain as the revolutions of the heavenly bodies. To believe otherwise is an admission of moral anarchy. That such a music of the moral spheres has yet to be revealed has failed to dissuade many that it does exist—we simply have not tried diligently enough to discover the perfect way, but as with the quest for peace and harmony among us, the goal lies just over the horizon.

The problem with this position is evident. If one accepts the strictures of an empirical theory of knowledge, then traditional assumptions of an absolute moral order cannot be admitted in the realm of the scientifically verifiable. This does not mean that they may not exist; it does mean that their existence cannot be proven. Indeed, precisely because of this fact, moral orders presumed to be founded on divine reasons or wills have never been universally satisfactory, that is, generally accepted or acceptable. Hence, what has been most troublesome to the absolutist mentality is the seeming lack of consensus in human value systems through the ages as to what constitutes justice. Yet if we view ourselves and our history from the vantage of organic evolution and the biology of our being, then what is revealed is a thoroughly constant and universal expression of justice. In its rudest, most basic, and elemental expression, it is that which promotes survival and reproductive success—and, that is what *Homo sapiens* has consistently preferred and sought. What ought we to do? That which most conforms with our most primal preference, our survival. What have we consistently done, that is, much more often than not? Precisely those things which we have intuited or determined as the appropriate means to this end. Have our choices always been accurate? By no means, but we have always referred our notion of justice to them. Some reflections and examples should clarify what I intend, a view of justice which is universally verifiable.

The notions of justice and law are so intertwined that the former cannot be discussed without some reference to the latter. We are all familiar with the law in its various formal aspects. It is the body of objective rules and regulations that serve as the day-to-day guides for our human activity. We make, break, amend, and void laws. We create a whole system of enforcement, litigation, and interpretation of law, the presence and continuity of which we largely take for granted. We speak of equality under the law and governments "of law, not of men," to signify the impartiality and objectivity of our legal structures. And we even debate whether or not certain laws are just or unjust, as though they actually possess this ultimate criterion as a quality.

Several characteristics of law are pertinent to my view of justice. Among its various functions is its role as a predictor of human action. Law both prescribes, in directing what ought to be done (paying one's taxes), and proscribes, by forbidding under threat of sanction certain other actions (exceeding a posted speed limit). In both instances laws are designed to, and if obeyed, serve to, make everyone's behavior in the community predictable. The confidence which we exhibit in proceeding through a street intersection when the traffic light is green is born of an assumption that those to whom a red light is showing will stop. So too, the explicit threat of punishment for not complying with the law is tantamount to a prediction of what action may be expected for its violation. It is clear that custom and convention, the informal siblings of statute rules, share in the predictive role.

Laws also exhibit a feature that is often overlooked or misunderstood. They discriminate in the sense that they establish distinct categories of persons, and as such are purposely designed to distinguish who and what shall be equal to whom and what, under specific circumstances. A vital function of law, therefore, is a separation of citizens into appropriate groups according to certain criteria of expected behavior. Thus, traffic laws apply only to those to whom they are intended to apply—motorists, cyclists, pedestrians, that is, particular groups of persons, acting in a specific set of circumstances. To all but these categories, these laws are irrelevant. Laws apply variously, some to a small number, others to a much broader spectrum. In this sense alone, the law bestows equality by designating categories of those who shall be considered, in its eyes, to be equal to each other. Finally, of course, the "law" itself does not *do* anything at all, for it is merely the concrete expression of how we direct or agree to treat each other on an ongoing basis.

As stated earlier it is evident that justice involves a relationship, but a relationship of a special kind. In our effort to express the nature of this relationship, Plato's description is partially satisfactory in that it seems to involve harmony or balance. Others have expressed this as an awareness of fairness. I would put it simply as a recognition of appropriateness, that things are as they should be. I further suggest that our feeling of "all-rightness" is an awareness that involves several levels or stages of interlocking calculation, each stage linked to the other in an ascending manner of increasing importance. It may be viewed as a pyramid in which the individual, various blocks of stone fit together to form the finished edifice, all contributing to accomplish the ultimate summit. We may picture the building stones as human institutions, laws, and values, with justice as the mortar which binds the parts to complete the whole. Let me begin with the most basic block of all, the administration of the law.

The traffic law is clear and unequivocal. If one is driving an automobile, one is expected to stop at an intersection if the traffic light is red, and can proceed through it if the light shows green. Exceptions are allowed for emergency vehicles, but that is precisely what they are—exceptions to the rule. Motorists who ignore the red stop light put themselves and others in jeopardy for they have introduced the element of unpredictability into their relationship with other motorists. Cross traffic motorists expect those with the red light to stop; in view of this expectation they travel through the intersection on the green light; the danger of a crash of vehicles is likely. Those who do not obey the stop signal have clearly violated an important law of traffic safety, with no excusable reason for their action, and are therefore subject to arrest and sanction for their illegal action.

But suppose the violator is a prominent person, a well-known politician or athlete, and the arresting officer, after recognizing him or her allows them to go without a ticket solely on the basis of their prominence. There are no formal mitigating or exceptional circumstances to excuse the motorist's violation, and only arbitrary whim on the part of the policeman allows the violator to escape a ticket. The motorist has clearly and with intent broken the law and is arbitrarily saved from punishment by the decision of the arresting officer. Without doubt, our sense of justice, of fairness, of appropriateness is offended. Our response is anger that the offender should be allowed to escape without penalty, when we know full well that under similar circumstances we would not be excused. Our response is immediate and straightforward—an injustice has been done because equals have not been treated equally.

As motorists we are all equal—the law says so. Doctor, lawyer, Indian chief, white, black, male, female, Christian, Jew, twenty or sixty years old—it makes no difference. If we drive an automobile we are expected to stop at red lights. We are all equals in this respect at least, and as such the law must apply to us equally with no arbitrary exceptions. This is the meaning of equality under the law—to whom the law is intended to apply, it shall apply equally. Any deviation from this norm means that an injustice has been done, and indeed one extending beyond the violator who is excused. The police officer himself has violated the law which binds him to enforce it. He has abdicated his responsibility and should suffer penalty for his action. One injustice has bred another, and if the policeman escapes punishment by his superiors for his lapse, injustice is further compounded. Clearly, we demand that the law be administered or applied as it is intended.

But what of the law itself? Why should it be obeyed in

the first place? Granted that public consensus requires an even-handed enforcement of the law, what is it in that consensus that supports the existence of societal rules and regulations? The very fact that lawbreakers are held to deserve punishment implies that the law is generally acknowledged as serving a purpose and as such deserves compliance. In an ordered community, that is, one in which few laws are broken or challenged, the law itself is implicitly affirmed as appropriate or just—it is given the benefit of the doubt. Simply, it is perceived as promoting an accepted value that is part of the community's public morality.

The laws which govern the operation of motor vehicles—everything from speed limits and traffic signals to licensing requirements of age and skill—are nothing more than accepted means for achieving that which is a common value within a motorized society—the safe and efficient movement of motor traffic. No other reason could possibly justify the existence of and the willing adherence to the myriad traffic laws tolerated by a society such as ours. They are accepted as just laws because they conform to and facilitate a community-wide norm, namely, a desire for public safety.

A law is perceived as just because those subject to it accept it as a concrete expression of a norm which they hold, a value which they accept. And precisely the opposite is true of a law perceived as being unjust. In the 1960s a test case was made of a long-standing Virginia law which forbade inter-racial marriage. At this time sixteen states had antimiscegenation statutes on their books. A racially mixed couple were married by a Justice of the Peace, were arrested by the county sheriff, and convicted in the subsequent trial. The matter was finally decided by the United States Supreme Court (*Loving* v. *Virginia*, 1967), the Virginia law being found unconstitutional. The Court's decision here, as in numerous other cases relating to racial segregation during this era, was that the law was contrary to the values of the community, as those values were expressed and implied in the Constitution, and as the Constitution was to be understood *at that time*. The Court's determination clearly indicated that such a legal intrusion, based on a criterion of race, could not be justified. In effect, it violated the public morality.

Such was not always the case. These and the whole panoply of laws that institutionalized racial segregation in the United States until the 1960s were in complete conformance with the society's post-Civil War public morality. The decision in *Plessey* v. *Ferguson* in 1893 merely ratified the consensus that racial separation was permissible, even though the public morality would no longer tolerate formalized chattel slavery. In approximately 120 years, the value system of this community shifted from a general acceptance of the view that white racial supremacy justified black enslavement, to a view that formally, at least, all races were and should be considered equal. And through the development to this latter view, the laws accurately reflected the various stages from the former notion to the latter. Were these laws just? Since they conformed to the value consensus of the society's majority at various times, it must be conceded that they were considered to be so. But what of the justness of this public morality which supported them? Granting that the ultimate criterion for a society's judgment of the justness of its laws is the community's value system, is there any conceivable criterion for judging this standard in its turn, or does it stand alone, like Rousseau's General Will—always right? Cultural or moral relativism would seem to warrant just such a conclusion.

Human slavery is one extreme example of what we now consider inhuman action towards each other. But let us recall that our community-wide sensitivity to this practice is a mere century old, a very short time in human history, and that the eloquent defenders of the South's peculiar institution could and did cite Thomas Aquinas and Aristotle as proponents of natural slavery. Is it possible that our contemporary rejection of slavery is "right" and a two-thousand-year-old counter tradition is "wrong"? Or is the ascription of right and wrong to human value systems, to entire public moral complexes, a spurious thing in itself? In other words, ought we to conclude to moral relativism at the societal level, and agree with Hume's inference that justice resides in what the conventions and customs of the *polis* declare it to be at any given time?

One advantage of such a position, theoretically at least, could be greater toleration, for no individual or group could logically and persuasively claim to be in sole possession of moral rectitude. The dogmatism that has so often characterized the ideologically persuaded might be replaced by a milder, live-and-let-live attitude. And as the public morality gradually shifts to accommodate different values from those that were previously held, no remorse would be felt over inconsistency—what was considered proper yesterday was proper, even as its opposite may be today.

Such a view would also be comfortable in the light of cultural differences. A culture develops and elaborates a normative scheme consistent with its needs, and as needs change, so too will the culture's values. So long as the laws conform to cultural values, and are administered in equal fashion to equals, any further consideration of their justice would no longer be debatable. The culture's or society's public morality would be its own justification, its values' judge in their own case.

Let us recall that the epistemological model which I have chosen to follow in this study is a modification of Humean scepticism. My aim is an analysis of human nature and of human values which proceeds inductively. The empirical (scientific) method deals with sense-perceived data. As such, no matter how refined and discreet the experimentation, the ultimately induced generalities cannot *logically* possess an *absolute* truth value. But as we know, science need not and does not trouble itself on this point. A high degree of probability is quite sufficient for the day-to-day conduct of human affairs—even to placing human beings on the surface of the moon.

Of more critical importance, however, is Hume's consignment of human values to the level of subjective opinion. As such, no individual or communal norms can pretend to "accuracy" or "correctness" at the existential level. Indeed, to even use such terms in reference to morality is logically to mix apples and oranges—two different levels or dimensions of "truth" operate between facts and values. Though values are conjured from facts—experience is the basis of opinion—the very fact of evaluation is a nonrational procedure, and as such its truth-value or verifiability is entirely different from a mathematical proposition or a generality induced from objective reality, sensorily perceived. Hence, facts as data possess an independent reality from us, the experiencing subject; values on the other hand depend for their reality on us, the evaluating subject. As such, values are true or correct only insofar as they are accepted or judged to be so by us, the evaluators. Thus far I have been considering the content of values, the substance of human preference and opinion. There is, however, a sense in which values themselves are facts. If I say that one person is "good," another "bad," I am expressing a value judgment, a preference based on my own subjective criteria, my personal model of goodness or badness. Though the origin of my value is subjective, it is nevertheless an objective fact that I hold this particular value. So too, it is an observable, existential fact that a community holds certain values, though the reasons for the values' formation is purely subjective. Hence, we can declare as fact that the value system of early nineteenth-century America included an acceptance of human slavery. It is also fact that our value system no longer supports such an institution. In light of the logic of moral relativism, it is time to return to the heart of the matter, the quest for a universal standard of justice.

Quite simply, such an endeavor would seem fruitless, for any such standard would be of human contrivance and hence by definition subjective. Here we must pause and make a vital distinction between the terms "absolute" and "universal." If the former is defined as unchanging and limitless then the epistemology employed here would necessarily preclude an absolute standard of justice—if such a standard does exist, it can never be ascertained with certainty if one accepts the logical rigor of an empirical theory of knowledge. Such a standard may only be supposed, never proved, and so of no value, save as an intellectual aerobic.

But the notion of universality is quite different and must not be confused with absolute. When we say that something is universally true, or held, or present, we are expressing the result of our observation of the thing in question—we are referring to a generality which may admit of exception, but rarely. Thus we may conclude from our observation that there exists a universal taboo against incest in human societies. This does not mean that there do not exist exceptions to this generally accepted rule. In fact, exceptions do exist but are precisely that—exceptions. The several general normative principles that form the foundation of all human societies (do not murder, steal, or lie) fall into this category of universal, that is, general rules which may nevertheless sometimes be broken by individuals within a society (to their possible peril), or even by whole societies (most often to the detriment of the society). With such a distinction the search for a universal standard of justice may not be so futile after all, and in fact I have already obliquely stated it in the observation that justice as a perceived appropriate relationship ultimately involves that which promotes human existence and conduces to procreative success.

Even more so than slavery the human activity of arbitrary and systematic extermination of one group by another strikes us as patently unjust. Unlike war or capital punishment where life is forfeit because the community feels threatened from without or within, we place genocide in a special category of killing. Despite the claims of those who kill, we condemn them and identify with their victims as innocent of wrongdoing. Pleas for racial purity or superiority or manifest destiny do not persuade us that the targets deserve such a fate. Instead, we decry the slaughter itself as a crime—a crime against humanity, a crime against us.

The Nazi Holocaust remains the most vivid modern example of genocide, but it was not unique in our century. From the Turkish slaughter of the Armenians, through the extermination of the Russian Kulaks, to the mass killing of rival tribes in decolonized Africa, to organized bloodbaths in Southeast Asia and Latin America, the twentieth has been a genocidal century. The point is not that humans *do* this to one another since it is clear from our record that we are quite capable of homicide, and with relish to boot.

Rather we must remark on the fact that the objective verdict of the unaffected is invariably sympathy for and identification with the victim. Seeing the fate of the slain as possibly reflective of our own, given similar circumstances, the outside observer condemns the killers as perpetrators of atrocity. Our intuition screams out that a massive injustice has been done.

But according to logic, with emotion set aside, how can we presume to pass judgment on the tribal mores or public morality of another community? How can we invoke in the name of humanity a transhistorical, omnicultural standard of justice in the face of moral relativism? We obviously cannot unless there does exist indeed such a standard, one so fundamental to the species that it transcends moral parochialism, supercedes specific cultural codes, and expresses a universal, species-wide norm or preference. Self-preservation is that norm.

I do not believe that this statement will surprise many who read it, and I certainly do not intend to pass off as an original insight the observable and verifiable fact that most members of our species, if given a clear-cut choice, would prefer life to death. Our highly developed sense of our own mortality in itself sharpens our desire to take every means possible to avoid death and prolong life. Our very laws and lifestyles aim in this direction. What is not so obvious, however, is the relationship of this ubiquitous preference for survival to a universal sense of the "just."

If it is agreed that most humans, most of the time, have in the past and do in the present seek to survive, that is, avoid death, then this must be conceded as the most fundamental human priority. At the preconscious, biologically instinctive level, our reactions of fear, fight, and flight are means that serve this end; at the conscious level of ratiocination, where alternative modes of action are weighed, the "choice" is made to act toward this end. Self-preservation, therefore, is our value of values, that to be sought first as the *sine qua non* to all else, for without life, considerations of its quality or style are meaningless. To preserve life we practice politics, that ingenious human interplay to avoid the conflict inherent in our ambivert nature. From this primal and primary need and expression there flow the secondary values which I have discussed earlier, and dependent on them there follow the laws and institutions that regulate and promote our varied existences and polities. But at rock bottom, we seek first, and prefer most, to live.[53]

This which we recognize as a primary preference rooted in our biology can hardly be denied. That we are capable of reasoning to the better or best means to maintain our existence—that we can learn and consciously make choices —in no way mitigates the fact that the urge which we follow is as natural to our being as it is to every other animal.

If in addition to our instinctual abhorrence of danger and death, we perceive that our conscious contrivances of laws and institutions are ineluctably linked to this same preservation norm, then the conclusion follows that death is held to be the greatest injustice of all for it negates our most primary and primal preference.

A policy of genocide is based on a principle. The principle is that one human group may arbitrarily exterminate another group. But if such a principle were to be universalized, that is, accepted by the species as a whole, it would clearly contradict the species' primary preference for survival, since the two are incompatible and mutually exclusive: We cannot generally prefer our own preservation while simultaneously allowing to another (or claiming for ourselves) a preference for mutual annihilation.

The incompatibility of the genocidal principle with that of life preservation is further evident from the fact that no group claiming it as a right would accept it as a right applicable to itself. The record does not indicate a reciprocal willingness in principle by Nazis to be exterminated by Jews. Reminiscent of Kant, we can conclude that the principle of this action cannot be made a universal principle for the species so long as the members of the species primarily prefer life preservation.

The same argument it seems to me applies to the matter of human slavery. If our primary human preference is guaranteed safety of existence, it is followed in short order by the desire for freedom in that existence. A policy of involuntary servitude, a denial of physical and psychological freedom of one group by another, is just as clearly as genocide based upon a principle that cannot be universalized in the face of a general fundamental preference for freedom. As a contradiction of a universal value, slavery must be considered objectively unjust, as is genocide, regardless of the subjective justification that it has received by societies which have practiced it in the past. In both the cases of genocide and slavery the policies have been imposed by the stronger upon the unwilling weaker, coupled with the former's refusal to allow in principle that its victims could do likewise to it.

It is apparent then that there does exist an objectively demonstrable universal basis or norm for determining the ultimate limits of what human beings must logically judge, in light of their core preferences, as justice.

This outer limit is an equal or perhaps prior awareness of what is unjust. The traditional literature on this subject has been preoccupied with justice as a quality, as a prescriptive good or goodness, as in the substance of the "good life." What this perspective has largely ignored is the truth conveyed in the story of the person who is asked to explain his preference in art. He responds, "I can't tell you why, I just know I don't like it."[54] The criteria for the human response of abhorence or dislike are a real and present part of our evaluation process of persons, things, and events, but more often than not they are never systemized at the logical or conscious level. Nevertheless the inaptness, unfairness, or injustice of relationships is truly perceived. Our initial reaction to genocide and slavery is that they are *un*just policies. Upon reflection we may conclude that they are so because the principles or claims upon which they are based violate, or are inappropriate to, the prior preferences of life and freedom. Our initial perception, however, is a negative one.

Efforts to define the substance of justice have foundered for lack of consensus because humans have not reasonably agreed on what they want (and perhaps never will), but they have most certainly decided what they do not desire. Jefferson's amendment of Locke's famous expression is worth recalling. He identified human inalienable rights as life, liberty, and the pursuit of happiness. Though linked as co-equals for rhetorical purposes, they are really not so: "Life" and "liberty" are claims which are better discerned in their absence and can be identified objectively in their violation (for example, genocide and slavery); "happiness" (linked to the freedom of its pursuit), however, is a notion devoid of objective substance—it is a subjective determination of individuals to be variously defined by them. Safety of existence and freedom for body and mind are the priorities, the *sine qua non*'s, which if not secured make the pursuit of happiness meaningless. Indeed, if "happiness" involves anything to anyone it must be seen as preceded by life and liberty.

Human normative systems may thus be seen as models, not for the achievement of the "good" life but for the avoidance of the "bad" life, that is, a constantly threatened existence or even a secure one that is lacking in freedom. Further evidence of this lies in the prohibitory emphasis of the specific norms discussed in chapters five and six. Without exception they indicate what limits may *not* be crossed, what actions are not permitted. And, as already noted, they all relate to guaranteeing that condition in which life is secure, within a human community—the basic environment in which the organism can safely procreate.

With this perspective, another notion regularly linked with justice can be better understood—the concept of right. As Locke bequeathed to the Liberal tradition a one-dimensional view of rational man, so too, he equipped that creature with some kind of inherent due which ought not to be violated. Thus do we still speak of individuals possessing rights, as though they are things—like limbs and organs—with which we are born.

As ambiverts we are never individuals in anything but the genetic sense. We are born into and live our lives in interaction with our conspecifics, and as such declare certain relationships as hopeful expectations of human behavior. It is these expectations which are our rights, and they can never be logically construed as absolute.

To announce the posssession of a right is to make a claim against the future actions of others. These others must be conspecifics, other humans who can understand our claim and accept or reject it. Thus to claim a right to life is to state a desire not to be killed. Our wish will be granted if we are willing to reciprocate in kind. But in doing so we are limiting our actions—in this case homicide —against others. We are exchanging claims, or establishing a realm of mutual right and obligation. Failure to accept limitation of our own actions towards others will precipitate their denial of our claim towards them. Thus, since obligation is limitation, no right can be absolute since absolute means "without limitation." The notion of right inherently involves stipulated reciprocity. Rights and obligations are, therefore, two sides of the same coin, expressing two aspects of a human relationship.

In this light, the inalienable rights of Locke and Jefferson can be seen, not as statements of an absolute condition or quality, but rather as forceful recognitions of the basic reciprocal relationships that must be acknowledged among humans—a security of person, with sufficient freedom, to pursue one's goals, all within the confines and limitations of a political community. Subsidiary or "civil" rights (and obligations) will follow as derivatives and will have different forms within different communities. The fundamental rights and obligations of life and liberty are expressions again of our most valued preferences, abrogation of which we consider to be the greatest injustice.

Through the course of this discussion I have argued in terms of two polarities—moral absolutism on the one hand and moral relativism on the other. I have rejected the former as inescapably *a priori* and potentially ideologic, while accepting the latter perspective as the only logical alternative, if one seeks an empirical basis for human morality. The term "moral relativism" should not be construed in a haphazard or trivial sense, however, as meaning an open-ended potpourri of equally valid norms. Quite the contrary is the case. The truth appears to be that human value systems in general, and the notion of injustice in particular, are "relative" only in their temporal and spatial expressions as secondary and tertiary applications of their parent norms. Thus, not stealing, not lying, not murdering are the universal, objective norms which form the warp and weft of the human polity. They are constant, consistent, and as rigid as the organism from which they generate. But as that organism is also flexible and adaptable, so too will be the applications of these norms that it will make. It is at this level, in this dimension and with this understanding, that the term "moral" or "normative" or "cultural relativity" must apply. Humans are beings who constantly adjust their behavior and the rules guiding that behavior in terms of the exigencies of their social time and place. But these adjustments are precisely that—mere variations on the central theme of life preservation and extension.

The ultimate standard which I have posited, self-preservation, is of course, in its own right, relative, that is, capable of change. This must be so since human values are capable of change. Logically it is conceivable that the human species could consciously elect to exterminate itself. Our capacity to choose such a course is possible. In this sense, our ultimate preference is also relative. Until such time as this option is exercised, however, its antithesis remains the final standard against which we do, in fact, measure and determine the unjust.

If we view ourselves as a species that is part of the phylo-genetic continuum, then we must acknowledge certain degrees of homology with other animals. More than enough data exist pertaining to the physiological changes that occur in our own and other species to conclude that we as well as they react instinctively to personal (and societal) threat. For them and us, fight and flight are the followers of fear.

We enjoy the added advantage of a cerebral cortex, which among other capacities enables us to predict and forestall danger from within and without our species. So equipped, we can reason to ways to avoid danger and mortal conflict. The conflict-avoiding constructs that flow from our instinctual response mechanism are the human norms that guide our action with our conspecifics. Most of us, most of the time, avoid lethal violence and mortal danger. We do so because we wish to survive, and the rules devised through our coming to be human have served us well in this regard as a species. We have adapted them to different circumstances so that they have taken on different hues—but their primary colors have remained the same.

When we perceive or sense that others are abiding by the rules of nonthreatening behavior we confidently pursue our personal and group goals. Our lives are truly "in order." The word we have coined for such a status is "justice," but it is, in fact, a recognition of the absence of injustice.

Justice is, therefore, in final analysis, a perceived condition of order, harmony, appropriateness—an intuition of calculation that things are as they should be. In this view it is not a thing to be grasped, but rather a condition to be enjoyed. When perception proclaims its absence, a tocsin sounds within our being, warning that things must be made right again. In striving, therefore, to make certain that laws are administered equally to equals, that the laws themselves conform to our values, and that those values of our polity do not violate that final norm, the ultimate reference point, self-preservation, we are reacting to injustice. And in doing so, we are affirming our biology.

VIII

The Future Remembered

That reason, passion, answer one great aim;
That true self-love and social are the same;
That virtue only makes our bliss below;
And all our knowledge is, ourselves to know.

Alexander Pope
An Essay on Man

What we are as human beings remains to be fully discovered, but it is discoverable. As paleoanthropology and its numerous cognate sciences reveal more about our origins so too will cytology, endocrinology, behavior genetics, and dozens of other studies provide us with greater understanding of why we behave as we do. With this knowledge should come a new perspective of the range of freedom which we possess within the limitations imposed by our genetic inheritance. Hopefully, then, the false dichotomy between nature and nurture can be finally laid to rest. A recognition that our human value systems, our public moralities, are the articulations of biologically based instincts for survival, and that they have played a major role in our attaining our present evolutionary status, will also mark a major intellectual gain. In turn, this should provide a clearer moral framework within which to formulate realistic public policy.

As we come to comprehend ourselves as beings which are free within limits, and discern with more precision what those limits are, the extremes of biological and environmental determinism can be exposed for what they are—one-dimensional, incomplete views of human nature which correspond only to a partial reality. The real task of understanding ourselves can then be pursued. Quite simply, that task is the discovery of what precisely are the biological, heritable structures and limitations within which we really can and do exercise freedom for alternative design of ourselves and our environment. If human behavior is perceived as neither wholly determined by genes or environment nor solely the result of "rationally" directed volition, but rather a complex interaction of all these factors, then the way in which we attempt to plan our future will be radically different than what it is at present. In this respect, our future will depend upon our knowledge of our nature—our prologue is, indeed, in our past.

The policy implications of this altered perspective are legion. I will mention only a few here by way of example. It must first be admitted that we are a naturally aggressive animal who will respond violently in order to protect his territory, and that security of territory is a prerequisite to personal survival and the production of the species' future generations. Organized, lethal conspecific violence, what we call war, is not an aberration of the species nor is it a vice. It is a distinctively human activity resulting from our big brain ability to forestall a future perceived threat by permanently eliminating an enemy. As a species it is part of our evolution. While this may seem a dismal conclusion, let us recall that while our history is one of constant warfare among some of us, it is also one of consistent peace among most of us, most of the time. But so long as a stable, secure identifiable territory is felt by a group to be denied to it, just so long human beings will fight to attain it. The goal may be disguised within a religious or secular ideology, but it nonetheless remains. Hence, "wars" of liberation, of revolutionary expectations, or of defense are all struggles among or within societies to achieve the wherewithal of human existence, regardless of the idealized rhetoric in the name of which they are waged. Since it is unlikely that everyone will ever be fully satisfied that he or she has obtained this goal, organized violence will continue among societies, as it doubtless will also continue at the interpersonal level within societies.

Human violence then is the result of human beings doing

very human things to each other. When we seek to gain too much for ourselves or feel that others are denying too much to us, our ambivert nature reacts aggressively and we temporarily suspend politics—we cease agreeing to disagree. But our ability to agree nonetheless remains. Our enormously sophisticated means of destroying each other is balanced by a unique ability to compromise our differences. What other species possess as instinctual rituals of submission to avoid lethal violence is possessed by us analogously as politics—the capacity to rationally control or resolve conflict.

There is no question, therefore, that a species-destructive or damaging nuclear conflict can be avoided. The necessary instruments of political discourse and action are already firmly in place to achieve this goal. What is lacking is a genuine conviction on the part of the policy-making actors and their constituencies that the outcome of a nuclear war between the superpowers would really produce the tragic consequences which have been predicted. Most of us know, either by direct experience or vicariously, to some degree or another, what it is like to be oppressed, threatened, frightened, or deprived of that which we value and need. But only a handful in proportion to the world's population knows the reality of an atomic explosion. Since we generally plan in terms of what we know instead of what we can only imagine, our cost-benefit calculation continues to persuade us that threat can be met by threat and territories and values protected by a nuclear war—in short, that the risk is not as great as it has been pictured. I can come to no other conclusion on this matter. Since the species has not indicated a sudden reversal of its millions of years' preference for survival it must mean that its policy-controlling elite—at least—remains unconvinced that the species' survival is really in jeopardy. That I and others disagree is of little matter since we are obviously in a minority. Policy changes regarding nuclear armament policy will only occur when policymakers concur with those whom they represent that there may truly be no human values gained from a nuclear conflict. Stripped of rhetoric, nuclear arms policies are reducible to a single question—do they or do they not provide the peace and security for human existence which still appears to be the primary human preference? I leave it to others to provide their own answer.

This brief excursion into the matter of potential nuclear violence is merely intended as an example of how ideology can often mask the real reasons why we engage in intraspecific aggression. A perspective which recognizes and takes into account man's biological inheritance—and the means for its control—provides a much sounder and realistic basis for global policymaking. The same is true when we confront the task of properly ordering our domestic societies.

The range of questions and problems in contemporary societies are many, and vary in degree from one to another. Most of them take on a different hue, however, when approached from a biological viewpoint. By this I mean that social engineering or redesigning which does not first take into consideration the structure and limitations of the already existing human biological design will simply not succeed. Male children will not be made more docile by giving them soft, cuddly toys instead of blocks to play with as infants—their nervous systems are "wired" differently from females, at least in infancy.[55] In this, as in so many other instances, we are discovering that certain human behavior patterns, while not "determined" in the now archaic sense of that term, are at least innately "projected." Environment and conditioning most certainly affect behavior but in a process of mutual interaction within an already given set of parameters. Male and female hormones are different, their brains and nervous systems are different, their musculature, skeletons, and chemical compositions are different—why is it surprising that, in the face of the same environment, their reactions and behavior will also be different? Other questions, unanswerable at this time but obviously related, come to mind. Why, for example, do males and females reach their respective sexual "peaks" at such disparate ages? What is the evolutionary advantage provided by the physiology of human sexuality? What effect have these and other unique characteristics played in the equally unique form of human bonding, the overlengthy maturation process of human offspring and myriad other related phenomena? And what can answers to these and other questions tell us about the limits to policymaking which intimately affect the human desires for offspring and territory? Designs for population control or the redistribution of property in the name of the "public good," which fail to take account of these basic human drives, will continue to be ineffectual and unsuccessful in the long run.

Without doubt the most startling and potentially important modern engineering project to date is not a social one in the usual sense. Genetic engineering has captured the attention of most of us for the implications which it portends. We can now redesign existing life and create entirely new life. We can screen for heritable defects and, in an increasing number of instances, remove those genetic factors which we deem undesirable. And with this technical ability we have authored a new catalogue of value questions and policy alternatives.[56]

The list of hitherto regarded behavior abnormalities which we now understand to have biochemical, heritable origins is growing at an almost daily rate. From schizophrenia to alcoholism, psychotherapy is giving way to biotherapy and our whole definition of disease is changing. What was once thought due solely to "moral lapse," degeneracy, bad upbringing, poor environment, and the like is now perceived as the result of a combination of factors, not the least of which is biological. These findings and the others which are certain to follow require a thorough reassessment of how we should view and deal with each other. Nowhere is this more evident than in the matter of homosexuality, which along with female prostitution, has a long history in our species, and which will no doubt before long be found to have a substantial biological component.

The point is that the biological revolution is in process of redefining before our eyes what we must understand as our nature, and hence what we will in turn call natural and unnatural about ourselves. In addition, with greater technical skills, we will possess an increasing ability to alter what we do not like about ourselves. A crucial question of genetic engineering, however, is how and why we will decide to alter those things which we do not like in ourselves and others. The most difficult and important questions will continue to center where they always have since we began to philosophize: What is the proper balance between individual need and social responsibility, between a self-defined personal dignity and a consensually determined common good.

The ability to ask these questions and to provide temporary and tentative answers is in itself a distinctively human characteristic. In terms of what we perceive, we claim as knowledge, and in the light of that knowledge, we frame queries of oughtness—the do's and don't's of our grand schemes and our everyday lives. Until the past few thousand years, we regulated our lives according to a handful of principles which unconsciously derived from an instinctual basis of survival and procreation. These standards served us well since most of our ancestors, most of the time abided by them. We are here today as witnesses to that fact and can retrospectively judge that we are fairly successful as a species. When our modern history began, and we codified the conventions and customs which were the secondary, derivative, variable cultural norms of our forebears, we perhaps began to take ourselves too seriously. We dogmatized and ideologized our parochial value systems —we wrote them in stone. In doing so we lost sight of that which we had never seen clearly but only sensed—that various value systems or public moralities were variations on the central themes and were "good" or "bad" only insofar as they conformed to or subverted those themes. When the planet filled up with humans, "alien" value systems necessarily clashed. Our innate fear of the strange and unpredictable was tapped and taxed as never before, and the simple truth that all of us seek the security of life and freedom—but in different ways—became obscured.

A recognition of this progressive loss of innocence as to the basis and function of human value systems is necessary as the pace of our knowledge expansion accelerates. An expanded understanding of what we are as organisms is increasing geometrically as is our capacity to reshape ourselves and our environment—of what we *can* become and do if we so choose. To the question of what we *ought* to do in the face of this ability we must have clearly in mind what the consequences will be in light of our fundamental preferences for life and its continuance, presuming that these values remain paramount. We no doubt will continue to seek what we will variously define as the good life, but the cart cannot come before the horse—a good life is premised upon life itself and is meaningless without it. We should better resign ourselves to the search for the "better" life, while recognizing that no group's vision of its own ideal can be justified at the expense of another's existence. This conclusion follows, of course, so long as the species continues to prefer that which it evidently has in the course of its evolution.

In final analysis I am proposing that there can be no philosophy of human nature without a science of human nature, and vice versa. Arguments about what we should do can only proceed from accurate knowledge of what we are truly capable of doing, and this truth can only come from science. In this essay I have referred to the new natural science of ethology as its practitioners describe it— the study of animals in their natural habitats, and in my prefatory remarks I mentioned my delight at the development of a new discipline, human ethology. Most expectantly I look forward to an enhanced realization by moral philosophers and natural scientists that the term *ethology*, in its traditional definition, already includes them both. Simply, it is described as "the science of ethics."

Notes

Introduction

1. An example of the increasing attention to this perspective among political scientists and its multidisciplinary application may be found in *Biology and the Social Sciences: An Emerging Revolution*, edited by Thomas C. Wiegele (Boulder, Col.: Westview Press, 1982).

2. This synthesis has been gaining momentum since the 1960s. An enormous amount of literature on the biological bases of human behavior is now in place, and most of the social sciences are represented by journals which deal either directly or indirectly with this theme. At the risk of giving offense to the others, I must single out for special mention one journal representing my own parent discipline of political science for its quality and comprehensiveness – *Politics and the Life Sciences*. Through its regular features and ongoing bibliographical updates it continues to be an indispensable tool for scholarship.

Though social scientists and humanists in greater numbers are turning their attention to the two decades of work by scholars in the "harder" of the life sciences, political philosophers, with but few, though notable, exceptions, have been slow to perceive the importance of this new field of study. This is surprising since human nature theory lies at the heart of the Western philosophical tradition, and the new knowledge of our being is so auspicious in its implications. It is therefore to this audience that the following essay is primarily addressed.

Note should also be made here of the forthcoming English translation of Irenaus Eibl-Eibesfeldt, *Biologie des menschlichen Verhaltens*, as *Human Ethology* (New York: Aldine de Gruyter, 1987). This is a long awaited book by one of the founders of the field of human ethology. The German edition is thrice reviewed in *Politics and the Life Sciences* 4:2, pp. 186–97.

I. The Query and the Quest

3. Renewed interest in the concept of human nature on the part of political philosophers is exemplified by the volume *Human Nature*

in Politics, ed. J. Roland Pennock and John W. Chapman (New York: New York University Press, 1977). Though criticized as a "popularizer" by many professional academics, the fact remains that the late Robert Ardrey accomplished his goal of stimulating interest in a redefinition of human nature from the perspective of evolutionary theory and ethological data. See especially his *The Territorial Imperative* (New York: Dell Publishing Co., Inc., 1966), and *The Hunting Hypothesis* (New York: Atheneum, 1976). The new direction towards an integration of science with philosophy has been indicated by Edmund O. Wilson, *On Human Nature* (Cambridge, Mass.: Harvard University Press, 1978). More than any other recent work, this remains the starting point for future philosophical discussion.

4. The works of Locke that are pertinent to my discussion are *An Essay Concerning Human Understanding,* containing his epistemological position, and *The Second Treatise of Civil Government,* in which he develops and contradicts his earlier outlined view of human nature and the social contract.

II. The Philosopher's Stone

5. For Plato's epistemology, see *Plato's Theory of Knowledge: The "Theaetetus" and the "Sophist" of Plato,* translated, with a running commentary, by Francis M. Cornford (Indianapolis, Ind.: Liberal Arts Press, Inc., 1957). For Aristotle's appropriate works on epistemology, plus commentary and annotated bibliography, see Fredrick Copleston, S.J., *A History of Philosophy, Vol. I, Greece and Rome* (Westminster, Md.: The Newman Press, 1955).

6. René Descartes, *Discourse on Method* and *Meditations on First Philosophy,* trans. Donald A. Cress (Indianapolis, Ind.: Hackett Publishing Company, 1980).

7. David Hume, *An Enquiry Concerning Human Understanding,* and *Dialogues Concerning Natural Religion,* in *The English Philosophers from Bacon to Mill,* edited with an introduction by Edwin A. Burtt (New York: The Modern Library, 1939). See also, *David Hume's Political Essays,* edited with an introduction by Charles W. Hendel (Indianapolis, Ind.: The Liberal Arts Press, Inc., 1953).

8. Locke, *Second Treatise.*

9. On the methodology of epistemology and a lengthy discussion of the "is"–"ought" problem and its relationship to moral discourse, see Paul W. Taylor, *Normative Discourse* (Englewood Cliffs, N.J.: Prentice-Hall, Inc., 1961).

10. See, for example, R. C. Lewontin, Steven Rose, and Leon J. Kamin, *Not In Our Genes: Biology, Ideology, and Human Nature* (New

York: Pantheon Books, 1984). "Reductionism," as a term of opprobrium, is used frequently by these authors to discredit sociobiology and any other variety of biologically oriented human nature theory or investigation which they deem to be "biological determinism." Their critique is curious, coming as it does from an avowedly Marxist perspective, a vantage often prone to the errors of the "naturalistic fallacy" which they intend to excise. For a fuller discussion of this point and their general argument, see my review in *Politics and the Life Sciences* 4:2, pp. 202–204.

III. In Search of the Beast

11. Charles Darwin, *The Origin of Species* (New York: New American Library, 1958); *The Expression of the Emotions in Man and Animals* (Chicago: University of Chicago Press, 1965); and *The Descent of Man* (Detroit, Gale Research, 1974). On Darwin, his age, and his intellectual precursors and contemporaries, see Peter Brent, *Charles Darwin* (New York: Harper & Row, 1981); Loren Eiseley, *Darwin and the Mysterious Mr. X* (New York: E. P. Dutton, 1979); Arnold C. Brackman, *A Delicate Arrangement* (New York: Times Books, 1980).

12. On "gradualism" and "saltationism," see the excellent summary of the seminal work by Stephen Jay Gould and Miles Eldredge in Gordon Rattray Taylor, *The Great Evolution Mystery* (New York: Harper & Row, 1983). This work is also useful for its discussion of the history of fossil evidence and the relationship of genetics to modern questions and problems in evolutionary theory.

13. James D. Watson, *The Double Helix* (New York: New American Library, 1968).

14. A sampling of the literature on fossil evidence of primate evolution includes W. E. LeGros Clark, *History of the Primates* (Chicago: University of Chicago Press, 1963); L. S. B. Leakey, *Adam's Ancestors* (New York: Harper & Row, 1960); Richard E. Leakey and Roger Lewin, *People of the Lake* (New York: Avon Books, 1979); and Richard E. Leakey, *The Making of Mankind* (London: Abacus, 1981); Donald Johanson and Maitland Edey, *Lucy: The Beginnings of Humankind* (New York: Simon and Schuster, 1981). Richard Leakey and Donald Johanson continue to make remarkable fossil discoveries in East Africa. True to its title, and an indispensable work on the unity of modern, evolutionarily pertinent, sciences, is *The Evolutionary Synthesis*, ed. Ernst Mayr and William B. Provine (Cambridge, Mass.: Harvard University Press, 1980).

15. As a major reinforcement of evolutionary theory, geochemistry

has taken its place with other sciences. See, for example, James E. Lovelock, *Gaia: A New Look at Life on Earth* (Oxford: Oxford University Press, 1979), and the elegant models of ancient atmospheres developed by Robert Berner, Antonio Lasaga, and Robert Garrels reported in *Science '85* 6:8, pp. 53 ff.

16. See, for example, M. C. Wittrock, *et al.*, *The Human Brain* (Englewood Cliffs, N.J.: Prentice-Hall, Inc., 1977); Richard Restak, *The Brain* (New York: Bantam Books, 1984); and, David H. Hubel, "The Brain," and F. H. C. Crick, "Thinking About the Brain," in *Scientific American Offprint,* "The Brain," (1984).

17. For this, as well as other issues discussed in this chapter, see Melvin Konner, *The Tangled Wing: Biological Constraints on the Human Spirit* (New York: Holt, Rinehart and Winston, 1982).

18. Graham Bell, *The Masterpiece of Nature: The Evolution and Genetics of Sexuality* (Berkeley, Calif.: University of California Press, 1982).

19. One of the most comprehensive works to date on the links between evolution, genetics, and human behavior remains, Theodosius Dobzhansky, *Mankind Evolving* (Toronto: Bantam Books, 1970).

20. Scientific opinion may never agree to what extent our prehuman ancestors were meat eaters. Though incontrovertible evidence may remain elusive, the argument from nutritional needs in Ardrey's *The Hunting Hypothesis* is very compelling. See also, Lionel Tiger, *Men in Groups* (New York: Vintage Books, 1970); and Lionel Tiger and Robin Fox, *The Imperial Animal* (New York: Holt, Rinehart and Winston, 1971). Related and other discussions are in Peter C. Reynolds, *On the Evolution of Human Behavior: The Argument from Animals to Man* (Berkeley, Calif.: University of California Press, 1981), and Branko Bokun, *Man: The Fallen Ape* (Garden City, N.Y.: Doubleday & Company, Inc., 1977).

21. Two works, which more than redress the balance in an otherwise "male dominance" perspective of early, prehuman familial and social bonding, are Sarah Blaffer Hrdy, *The Woman That Never Evolved* (Cambridge, Mass.: Harvard University Press, 1981), and Helen E. Fisher, *The Sex Contract* (New York: William Morrow and Company, Inc., 1982). The latter, for example, is a well-reasoned reconstruction in light of the available evidence of the emergence of human familial bonding and by extension, group socialization, based upon the centrality of the unique adaptiveness of human female sexuality.

22. "Inclusive fitness" and "reciprocal altruism" are two related terms which now occupy central positions in the sociobiological and cognate literature, the theories of biologists William Hamilton and Robert Trivers, respectively. Complementary theories, they seek to explain altruistic, even self-sacrificing behavior, in terms of kin-

selection and genetic survival. Thus, cooperation among related individuals would serve to heighten the preservation of one's own genes (physical immortality) through the dispersed but accumulated genes of one's siblings, offspring, and near relatives. A cost-benefit calculus would favor the evolution of altruistic behavior, with the evolutionary selection process tending to eliminate or at least mitigate the continuation of consistent deceitfulness and betrayal. Richard Dawkins, *The Selfish Gene* (Oxford: Oxford University Press, 1976) brought these ideas to a wide and general audience. Dawkins, in *The Extended Phenotype* (Oxford: Oxford University Press, 1982), and, C. J. Lumsden and E. O. Wilson in *Genes, Mind, and Culture: The Coevolutionary Process* (Cambridge, Mass.: Harvard University Press, 1981), have extended these notions further in the linkage between biological and cultural evolution. For an extensive review of the literature, plus an application and extension of these theories, see Gary R. Johnson, "Kin Selection, Socialization, and Patriotism: An Integrating Theory," *Politics and the Life Sciences* 4:2 (1986), pp. 127–154, with commentaries by Francis A. Beer, Pierre L. van den Berghe, and J. Phillipe Rushton. These theories are supportive of my following discussion in chapters 5 and 6 on the biological basis of human normative principles, especially those relating to lying, stealing, and procreative integrity.

The question of whether the individual or the group is selected for in the process of natural selection, that is, species perpetuation, has been contested for some time. I do not feel that an eventual victory of one theory over the other would substantially alter the plausibility of my conclusions. If human beings are ambiverts, as I describe in the following chapter, then we are automatically individuals, members of a "kin-clan" as well as of various formal and informal social groups – all simultaneously a part of the species. The way in which we affect others and are in turn affected by them may be likened to a handful of gravel thrown into a pond: The individual stones make their own marks on the water surface but each causes ripples that intersect and impinge on many others. Individual persons most certainly retain contingent choice within the limits of their existential experience. It is the interaction of individual choices, in ever-increasing affectation and intermingling, that will eventually constitute a species-wide effect. Hence, to claim individual or group survival as more or less imperative is to isolate a literally nonisolatable phenomenon.

23. See Fisher, *The Sex Contract*, pp. 19–37, and the reference on innateness of flirting from Irenaus Eibl-Eibesfeldt, *Ethology: The Biology of Behavior* (New York: Holt, Rinehart & Winston, 1975).

24. Of special relevance to this and my later discussion is Konrad Lorenz, *On Aggression*, trans. Marjorie Kerr Wilson (New York: Bantam Books, 1967). This work not only brought to general attention

Lorenz's work in animal behavior, for which he shared the Nobel Prize in 1972 with Tinbergen and von Frisch, but also established him as the foremost exponent of an innate aggressive instinct in human beings. In *Behind the Mirror: A Search for a Natural History of Human Knowledge*, trans. Ronald Taylor (New York: Harcourt Brace Jovanovich, 1977), Lorenz develops the evolutionary basis of cognition. A bibliography of his publications, papers, and lectures to 1976 is in Alec Nisbett, *Konrad Lorenz* (New York: Harcourt Brace Jovanovich, 1976). Jane Goodall's pioneering work with wild chimpanzees is recounted in *In the Shadow of Man* (New York: Dell, 1971), and "Life and Death at Gombe," *National Geographic* 155:5. The late Dian Fossey's study of the Mountain Gorilla is in "The Imperial Mountain Gorilla," *National Geographic* 159:4. The most important recent work on chimpanzee life and behavior is Frans de Waal, *Chimpanzee Politics: Power and Sex Among Apes* (New York: Harper & Row, 1984).

25. See de Waal, *Chimpanzee Politics*; and, Sarah Blaffer Hrdy, *The Langurs of Abu: Female and Male Strategies of Reproduction* (Cambridge, Mass.: Harvard University Press, 1977).

26. See Goodall, "Life and Death at Gombe."

VI. *Ecce, Homo Politicus*

27. Aristotle, *Politics*, I, c. I, trans. Ernest Barker (London: Oxford University Press, 1952); *Nichomachean Ethics*, IX, c. IX and I, c. VII, trans. W. D. Ross (London: Oxford University Press, 1925). Though familiar, the entire argument of both works provides valuable insights for an evolutionary perspective of human nature and morality.

28. St. Thomas Aquinas, *Summa Theologica*, II-II, 78. A standard commentary on Aquinas is that of Etienne Gilson, *The Christian Philosophy of St. Thomas Aquinas*, trans. L. K. Shook (New York: Random House, 1956).

As the formal structure of the *polis* disappeared, so too did that appreciation of it as the locale of human ethos and pathos. Today that dimension of human relationships is only vaguely conveyed in the term "community."

29. This motif is present in many of Marx's writings but, see especially, Karl Marx, *Pre-Capitalist Economic Formations*, ed. E. Hobsbawm (London: Lawrence and Wishart, 1964); *The Marx-Engels Reader*, ed. Robert C. Tucker (New York: W. W. Norton & Company, 1972); *Karl Marx, Selected Writings*, ed. David McLellan (Oxford: Oxford University Press, 1977). For commentary, see Louis Dupré, *The Philosophical Foundations of Marxism* (New York: Harcourt Brace

Jovanovich, 1966), and Shlomo Avineri, *The Social & Political Thought of Karl Marx* (London: Cambridge University Press, 1976).

30. G. W. F. Hegel, *Philosophy of Right*, trans. T. M. Knox (Oxford: Oxford University Press, 1942).

31. Jean-Jacques Rousseau, *On The Social Contract*, ed. Roger D. Masters, trans. Judith R. Masters (New York: St. Martin's Press, 1978).

32. *Burke's Politics: Selected Writings and Speeches of Edmund Burke*, ed. Ross J. S. Hofman and Paul Levack (New York: Alfred A. Knopf, 1949).

33. See Dian Fossey, *The Imperial Mountain Gorilla.*

34. The literature on "dominance hierarchies" is growing apace with that devoted to other ethological models. A recent study on the role performed by bureaucracies as conflict control mechanisms is *Biology and Bureaucracy: Public Administration and Public Policy from the Perspective of Evolutionary, Genetic, and Neurobiological Theory*, ed. Elliote White and Joseph Losco (Lanham, Md.: University Press of America, 1986).

35. I have borrowed this term from Tiger and Fox, *The Imperial Animal*, as they use it in its ethological sense.

36. See Roger D. Masters, "Evolutionary Biology, Political Theory, and the Origin of the State," in *Law, Biology, and Culture*, ed. Margaret Gruter and Paul Bohannan (Santa Barbara, Calif.: Ross Erikson, 1983); and, "The Biological Nature of the State," *World Politics* 35: 161–193. In the past decade and a half, in numerous seminal works, Masters has pointed the way to an integration of traditional human nature theorizing with the evolutionary perspective. A sense of his contribution to the contemporary renaissance in political philosophy may be obtained from his retrospective article and following commentaries, "Human Nature and Political Theory: Can Biology Contribute to the Study of Politics?" in *Politics and the Life Sciences* 2:2, pp. 120–150.

37. *Homo sapiens* is therefore *Homo politicus*. We are the heirs of our forgotten genes while at the same time the vehicles of those very genetic transferences. Our continuation as a species involves and demands our attention to use our abilities to control our innate drives. But rational or reasoned concern for the alternatives which we present to ourselves has not necessarily provided us with the best results. For example, we have harnessed the power of the universe in nuclear fission and fusion but have yet to decide and to act to use this knowledge in a less than lethal way.

It is possible that Lorenz was partially correct when he speculated about the human brain "out-distancing" the evolution of conflict control rituals possessed by other animals. Be that as it may, we do not have automatic retarders or instinct suppressors to nearly the extent of other animals. But we do possess a brain which enables us to pick up that slack, to consider ends and means and to choose accordingly – and this, in turn, means that we are political.

V. The Normative Animal

38. The "nature versus nurture" controversy in its revived formulation dates from the early 1970s, prompted largely by the popularity of Lorenz's *On Aggression* and the enormous impact of the work of Edward O. Wilson. With the publication of *Sociobiology, The New Synthesis* (Cambridge, Mass.: Harvard University Press, 1975) and *On Human Nature*, Wilson has literally established a new academic discipline and himself as the foremost proponent of biological determinism, at least as that term is understood by his pro-nurture critics. These latter include a range of scholars from the natural and social sciences and the humanities, who would ordinarily have little in common. Thus, many Marxists and Feminists, philosophers and theologians, anthropologists and psychologists, and "humanists" of various persuasions and specialties criticize sociobiology for, at best, a lack of scientific rigor and at worst, a resurrection of Social Darwinism with definite class and racial overtones. It should be noted that those scholars, who are pursuing their own disciplines from a biological perspective (bio-politics, -history, -philosophy, to name only several), are often erroneously identified with sociobiology because they find genuine merit in a biological approach in their own studies and have genuine doubts about the continued accuracy and viability of the traditional social philosophies. These are the scholars to whom I earlier referred as in process of constructing the study of human ethology. One thing is certain – environmental determinism is fighting a rearguard action, the result of which will be an empirically reconstituted view of human nature. Of the vast literature available, the following are representative samples which I have not cited elsewhere: Ronald Fletcher, *Instinct in Man* (New York: Schocken Books, 1966), and Anthony Storr, *Human Aggression* (New York: Atheneum, 1968), early books which reenforced Lorenz's theses; *Man and Aggression*, ed. Ashley Montagu (London: Oxford University Press, 1973), essays attacking Lorenz and the above from the traditionalist position; *The Sociobiology Debate*, ed. Arthur L. Caplan (New York: Harper & Row, 1978), still a standard statement of the issues with over forty articles. Since the publication of Thomas L. Thorson's book, *Biopolitics* (New York: Holt, Rinehart and Winston, Inc., 1970), the study by this name has grown rapidly to the point where it is now recognized as a sub-

field within political science, and the largest of its kind among the social sciences. The Association for Politics and the Life Sciences, through its meetings and journal, *Politics and the Life Sciences*, focuses the research and publications of several hundred scholars internationally. In addition to his above cited *Biology and the Social Sciences*, the journal's editor, Thomas C. Wiegele, has authored an especially useful book for the teaching of biopolitics, *Biopolitics: Search for a More Human Political Science* (Boulder, Col.: Westview Press, 1979). Many traditional fields are now represented by journals and periodicals aimed at integrating them with biology and the life sciences. Among notable recent additions is *Biology and Philosophy*.

39. Marx's preference for English and French Socialism was directly related to his notion of the revolutionary character of *praxis*. See *The Holy Family*, and *Introduction to a Contribution to the Critique of Hegel's Philosophy of Right*.

40. The "two guises" to which I refer are the "liberal"-"conservative" distinction of popular political parlance. Both are, of course, variations of the "Anglo-Saxon Liberal" tradition, dating from Locke. An excellent case can be made that Marx's system owes as much or more to this tradition than to German Idealism. Marxism and Liberalism certainly both share naive assumptions and expectations with regard to the human being's ability to shed the strictures of its "animal nature."

41. For the story of American cultural determinism and the Boas, Benedict, Mead connection, see Derek Freeman, *Margaret Mead and Samoa, The Making and Unmaking of an Anthropological Myth* (Cambridge, Mass.: Harvard University Press, 1983). An example of the degree to which Mead's biases live on can be seen in the work of a contemporary cultural anthropologist, Colin Turnbull. He, too, has been seduced by the Liberal state of nature fantasy of natural man – this time symbolized by the Pygmies of the Ituri rain forest in Central Africa – while he is repelled by the disintegration of the human polity of the Ik in East Africa. Colin M. Turnbull, *The Forest People* (New York: Simon and Schuster, 1962) and *The Mountain People* (New York: Simon and Schuster, 1972).

42. The coincidence of human value systems at the primary level is evident from all the anthropological literature, as is their base for and incorporation into religious belief. The definitive work to date (and for the foreseeable future) on this subject is Weston La Barre, *The Ghost Dance: Origins of Religion* (New York: Dell Publishing Co., Inc., 1972). On the origins of the Old Testament, see also, Alexander Heidel, *The Gilgamesh Epic and Old Testament Parallels* (Chicago: University of Chicago Press, 1963), and *Origins: Creation Texts from the Ancient Mediterranean*, ed. and trans. Charles Doria and Harris Lenowitz (New York: Anchor Press/Doubleday, 1976). A classic of

this literature remains Sir James George Frazer, *The Golden Bough, A Study in Magic and Religion* (New York: Macmillan Publishing Co., Inc., 1963).

43. Recalling my discussion of Hume's critique in chapter two, the following discussion of the Decalogue should not be misunderstood as an attempt to derive "ought" from "is." Quite the contrary, I am in no way implying that its principles ought to be complied with (carry any prescriptive weight) merely because they have been in the past. They are viewed here as strictly functional means to achieving an end. If human preference (self-preservation) remains the same, they may still serve their past purpose. My contention here and following is that the more we appreciate how and why we have arrived at our present moral paradigm, the greater will be our understanding of the limits of our future moral choices.

44. Ludwig Feuerbach, *The Essence of Christianity* (New York: Harper & Bros., 1957); Sigmund Freud, *The Future of an Illusion* (New York: Doubleday & Co., Inc., 1964).

> Naturalistically approached, human religion turns out to be an *entirely* human phenomenon, and entirely derived from the nature of human nature. Religion has never been explainable in the terms provided by religion, and the long search for knowledge of the gods or of God has given us no knowledge whatever that is acceptable to all men. Why not then look carefully at man himself for an understanding of this human phenomenon? It may startle those who would find God to be asked first to look at Australopithecine apemen. La Barre, *The Ghost Dance*, p. xi (author's emphasis).

45. One of the best syntheses on the biological bases of human behavior and emotions is Melvin Konner, *The Tangled Wing*. Konner's thoroughly dispassionate approach and elegant argumentation should be viewed as the foundation for an "interactionist" position on the relationship of biology and human nature theory. The nature-nurture dichotomy should now die a natural death.

46. See Wilson, *On Human Nature*, chapter 8, "Religion."

VI. The Self-Serving Species

47. It is obvious that, despite protestations to the contrary, the Christian notion of a triune deity is perilously close to polytheism, while belief in a virgin mother echoes the *Bona Dea* or Good Goddess of the Romans, itself a derivative of more ancient Mediterranean "Earth Mother" belief.

48. The naturalistic ethic developed here has some precedence in the thought of Darwin and Herbert Spenser, but should not be con-

fused with them, especially the latter (see, for example, Wilson, *On Human Nature*, pp. 224-225). More recent work which supports my view in whole or in part includes, in addition to Wilson, Fisher, Hrdy and Konner, already cited, the following: Julian S. Huxley, *Evolution and Ethics* (London: Pilot Press, 1947); C. H. Waddington, *The Ethical Animal* (London: Allen & Unwin, 1960); Antony Flew, *Evolutionary Ethics* (London: Macmillan, 1967); Robin Fox, *The Red Lamp of Incest* (New York: E. P. Dutton, 1980); Marvin Harris, *Cannibals and Kings* (New York: Random House, 1977); George Edgin Pugh, *The Biological Origin of Human Values* (New York: Basic Books, Inc., 1977); and J. L. Mackie, *Persons and Values: Selected Papers*, volume II (Oxford: Oxford University Press, 1985). I am indebted to Michael Ruse for this last citation (*Biology and Philosophy* 2:2 [1987], p. 229). See, also, his *The Philosophy of Biology* (London: Hutchinson, 1973); and Bernhard Rensch, *Biophilosophy*, trans. C. A. M. Sym (New York: Columbia University Press, 1971). As the present work was going to press an important new study was published which deserves much greater attention than can be afforded here. Richard D. Alexander's *The Biology of Moral Systems* (New York: Aldine De Gruyter, 1987) is a state of the art argument for the biological bases of human normative systems. An evolutionary biologist, he provides supportive evidence for many of the conclusions that I draw, as well as providing different emphases on issues which we both consider to be crucial (e.g., the nuclear arms race).

49. Traditionally, even acknowledged children of concubines had no claim to the name or inheritance of their fathers, though those like a King Solomon or a Turkish sultan were wealthy enough to support the additional mothers and children. In this vein, the fact that harems were guarded by eunuchs guaranteed that no specious pregnancies could take place among the sultan's wives or concubines – though sexual activity most assuredly could and did.

50. Two now dated but still useful studies of warfare are Maurice R. Davie, *The Evolution of War* (Port Washington, N.Y.: Kennikat Press, Inc., 1968), and Quincy Wright, *A Study of War* (Chicago: University of Chicago Press, 1965). Also useful as a literature guide is William Tulio Divale, *Warfare in Primitive Societies, A Bibliography* (Santa Barbara, Calif.: Clio Press, Inc., 1973). The single most important work in recent years for the purpose of my discussion is Irenaus Eibl-Eibesfeldt, *The Biology of Peace and War: Men, Animals, and Aggression*, trans. Eric Mosbacher (New York: The Viking Press, 1979). For an example of an historical attempt to normatively control the violence of warfare, see Richard Shelly Hartigan, *The Forgotten Victim: A History of the Civilian* (Chicago: Precedent Publishing, Inc., 1982).

51. Every so-called capital sin (lust, greed, etc.) is nothing more than an extreme of a perfectly natural inclination – it becomes reprehensible when considered dangerous to the community.

VII. The Biology of Injustice

52. The traditional literature on the notion of justice, from Plato and Aristotle, through Augustine and Aquinas, to Marx, John Stuart Mill and T. H. Green, is familiar enough. Two recent, and fundamentally opposing systematic studies, are Arnold Brecht, *Political Theory – The Foundations of 20th Century Political Thought* (Princeton, N.J.: Princeton University Press, 1959) and John Rawls, *A Theory of Justice* (Cambridge, Mass.: Belknap Press, Harvard, 1971). Most recently, Michael Walzer, in his *Spheres of Justice* (New York: Basic Books, Inc., 1983) develops the notion of distributive justice in terms of equality and pluralism. An excellent introduction to contemporary but pre-biopolitical approaches to various aspects of the question is *Justice*, ed. Carl J. Friedrich and John W. Chapman (New York: Atherton Press, 1963). For a biophilosophical, evolutionary perspective, see Roger D. Masters, "Evolutionary Biology and Natural Right" in *The Crisis of Liberal Democracy: A Straussian Perspective* (Albany, N.Y.: State University of New York Press, 1986) and "Political Philosophy as a Science: Evolutionary Biology, Political Theory, and Natural Justice," paper presented at the annual meeting of the American Political Science Association, Washington, D.C., 1986.

53. Instances of individual or mass suicides or voluntary martyrdoms in no way vitiate the universality of the survival preference. Indeed, they are noteworthy precisely because they are extraordinary.

54. Also consider the comment of United States Supreme Court Justice Potter Stewart in the case of *Jacobellis* v. *Ohio* (1964): "I shall not today attempt further to define the kinds of material I understand to be embraced within that shorthand description /of hard-core pornography/ . . . But I know it when I see it. . . ." From the text of the decision, in Gerald Gunther, *Constitutional Law*, 11th edition (Mineola, New York: The Foundation Press, Inc., 1985), p. 1072.

VIII. The Future Remembered

55. See Konner, *The Tangled Wing*, chapter 6, for an extended discussion of the data on gender differences. See also, Diane McGuiness, "How Schools Discriminate Against Boys," in *Human Nature* 2:3, pp. 82–88. The data is multiplying at an ever-increasing

pace demonstrating the links among genes, hormones, and behavior predispositions.

56. Nowhere in contemporary science research and its attendant technology is there such an "ethical gap" as in the province of genetic engineering. My own feeling is that the confusion and ambivalence demonstrated by scientists, ethicists, and policymakers as to what "ought to be done, what avoided, what prohibited," is due largely to the fact that science is raising fundamental questions about our human nature, questions that cannot be satisfactorily answered in terms of traditional moral paradigms, based as these are on obsolete or incomplete definitions of that nature. A brief sample of attempts to outline the issues and/or provide temporary and partial solutions includes: Robert T. Francoeur, *Utopian Motherhood* (New York: A. S. Barnes and Co., 1977); Philip Reilly, *Genetics, Law, and Social Policy* (Cambridge, Mass.: Harvard University Press, 1977); Andrew C. Varga, *The Main Issues in Bioethics* (New York: Paulist Press, 1984); and, Robert H. Blank, *The Political Implications of Human Genetic Technology* (Boulder, Col.: Westview Press, 1981). An indispensable tool for any discussion of these issues is *The Social Impacts of Biotechnology: An Annotated Bibliography of Recent Works*, ed. Thomas C. Wiegele (DeKalb, Ill.: The Association for Politics and the Life Sciences, 1986). An introduction to modern genetic research and some of its policy implications is Dr. Zsolt Harsanyi and Richard Hutton, *Genetic Prophecy: Beyond the Double Helix* (New York: Bantam Books, Inc., 1982).

Index